The Day I Got Sectioned

Liz Green

First published in 2018 by Liz Green Bank Lane, Upper Denby

Text © Liz Green 2018

ISBN: 978-1-78926-418-0

Printed and bound in Great Britain by

CPI Group (UK) Ltd, Croydon CR0 4YY

Cover photograph © Liz Green

Cover artwork and typesetting by Helen Stothard
hmsdesign@btinternet.com

Contents

Introduction

It could happen to any of us.

We hope it won't.

We do our best to 'keep it together'.

That's what I did, but after a very stressful period in my life and a serious lack of sleep, it happened to me.

I woke up in a mental hospital.

I was sectioned under the Mental Health Act.

It wasn't as simple as that, it was an unravelling of my life and the lives of those around me at the time. I'll share more on the pages that follow.

I had one of the most terrifying experiences of my life. The world wasn't ending, no-one had died, world war III hadn't started, knife wielding crazy folk weren't running around my village trying to kill everyone but my mind told me differently.

Life became very surreal. Like I was in a movie or on a really twisted game show fighting for my survival. I was scared, I felt unsafe, I felt out of control, like no-one understood what was happening and I couldn't control anything anymore. Like no-one was hearing me or understanding me, at one point I wondered if I had died and was simply a lost soul floating around trying to be heard. I was beyond terrified!

My whole world fell apart. Now it's time for me to put it back together again and share my story. I will speak my truth, I will have strength and courage from within this vulnerable and sometimes shameful space, I cannot unsee what I have seen. It broke my heart wide open.

I share this story from my heart to yours, as part of my own personal healing journey and yours too. Maybe you have experienced mental health issues first hand or supported someone through their own journey and experience of 'losing it'. However you came to be reading this book I hope what I share will make a difference to the way the world is set up and also bring clarity and understanding of what a mental breakdown can feel like first hand.

I have a calling.

The call has been answered.

Everything shared in this book is from my own perspective, nothing is meant to cause any offence, most involved were simply doing their best. I too am simply doing my best as I share what follows, I have chosen to self-publish this book to start with as I want to get my story out into the world ASAP. I hope through publicity, sharing my story and having support from all of you that this can happen. My focus is to share as openly and honestly as possible being as transparent as I can, in integrity, integrating it all.

Due to the nature of the circumstances and my breakdown, as well as the medication I was administered, my perspective may not always be exactly how things unfolded. I will do my best to share what happened, through my words and stories, in such a way that you can get a really good feel for what I experienced.

Not everyone involved were 'baddies', some of the nurses, staff, advocates and practical support I received was very helpful and is greatly appreciated. To be fair on many occasions it wasn't the people who were the issue it's the mental health system they are caught up in. Fire fighting and doing the best of a bad job.

Thank you to everyone who helped me, you know who you are and I appreciate you.

My intention is to manifest a Publisher who is willing to support this book and its birth into the wider world so it can reach even more people globally and hopefully make a difference to this old and very much outdated system I was stuck in.

I will do all that I can to help this cause.

I will share my story.

I have a favour to ask you.

Please do your best to ignore any grammatical or spelling mistakes. It's only been a short while since my release so I am still healing. My main aim is to get this book out there and available to read. I appreciate you being here reading this and welcome any further support you could offer too.

Hopefully soon it will be given some magic and sparkle from a wonderful Publisher and will also be available in book shops around the world. I did contact a couple of publishers but they said I needed a literary agent, I will keep going.

For now it's just me and my 10-year old laptop.

Here goes. My story.

Shared with love and an open heart,

Liz

CHAPTER 1

Out Of The Frying Pan Into The Fire

When I look back I'd been out of my routine for a month or so beforehand, caring for a friend who'd had an operation, giving too much of myself (lesson learnt!). It's so hard when you find yourself in a situation like that, I'm certain you will have experienced your own version of giving too much of yourself and the exhaustion it can bring.

Things went from bad to worse when she started to suffer with her own mental health issues, it took a week for her to be sectioned and get the medical support required. This is not my story to share but I have to set the scene.

I went for days without sleep. I saw some really upsetting and unsettling things. These things triggered me, if I had slept more and wasn't in that situation maybe I would have felt differently. Without going into too much detail about someone else's story I felt scared for everyone's safety.

I'd spent most of the week before my own breakdown asking "Are you safe?" "Is she safe?" "Are the kids safe?" "Is everyone safe?"

We had created a messenger group online to keep everyone involved in the loop, basically all doing our best in a very difficult situation.

I felt like a puppet on a string going back and forth trying to 'fix' everything and hold it together. I know everyone involved has their own version of what happened but for me it all became too much.

You see I also have my own health issues to deal with, 10 years ago I was diagnosed with Meniere's disease. It's nothing life threatening but it's not very nice. Deafness, vertigo attacks, dizziness, disorientation and such like. I had it pretty much under control but for me to remain healthy well and balanced I require routine.

I was completely out of any routine. Also to add to the pressure the weekend all of this stuff kicked off I was having a new boiler fitted too so my lovely little cottage was covered in brick dust and I didn't have any hot water. Magical, relaxing baths are an important part of my routine too.

After six days of worry, stress and not very much sleep at all I decided to take a step back from the vortex of manic energy which felt really out of control at this point. I booked myself into the doctors to make sure I had my Meniere's medication as I started to feel really off balance at this point.

At first they told me it would be a few weeks until I could have an appointment, I knew I needed one much sooner and managed to get in the following day.

It turns out the doctor I saw was the same one who had assessed my friend a few days ago and she had put me down as a point of contact, so the appointment I had booked ended up being about that. At this point I could already feel myself spiralling out of control so this only added to my stress.

Especially when I relayed some of the stuff I was worried about and the doctor told me a story about when he once visited a mental health patient who told him he was DOCTOR DEATH!

The main trigger for me was a hunting knife I saw at my friend's house. Until this point I didn't really know a knife would be such a big trigger, also the real fire which was once a source of comfort on a cold winter's day became something to be feared in case anyone got hurt as more and more things were thrown into the flames.

As you can imagine the Dr Death comment really didn't help at this point. Neither did the eye-rolling and disinterest from the doctor. Also being told there was nothing any of us could do unless someone was in danger. I was told that's when we could call 999 to force the inevitable to happen.

I was at the top of my tree!

I could feel myself on the edge of a very thin ledge and simply could not wrap my head around what was happening.

At the time I was saving all of the messages and texts I had been sent during this week in case anyone involved ended up getting injured or killed. I was getting calls, messages and texts even after I took a step back from the group, I was still in the thick of it.

I had all this stuff swimming around my head worrying about what I imagined might happen, on a practical level I was also still getting calls and messages until the early hours of Friday 13th (I know ironic isn't it!). That's when I spoke to another friend involved, she was locked in the bathroom whispering she had called the police, she was OK but in my mind things were seriously fucked up now. I wondered why she had locked herself in the bathroom and imagined the worst. I called the police too. I told them what I had seen a few days earlier, my voice was shaking so hard I struggled to get my words out and contain my fear at this point. I was afraid someone would get hurt or my friend would hurt herself.

That's when things really started to flip.

I didn't feel like myself at all.

I couldn't settle.

I couldn't sleep.

My head was racing with fear and panic.

Had someone died? Was everyone safe? Was I safe? Was the world safe?

I'd been relaying all of the messages, texts and conversations to my chap, as well as everything I was experiencing and feeling. He hadn't had much sleep either and he was sick of hearing about it. I was feeling sick to the pit of my stomach talking about it.

He was shocked by what had unfolded but knew we needed sleep. He was worried I was making myself ill. Which I was.

Sleep what's that again?

The events of that weekend, before my sectioning, was totally out there! Friday the 13th certainly wasn't a lucky one for me that's for sure!

I didn't know whether to laugh or cry.

I think the medical term for what I experienced is psychosis, this came from some online research as I wasn't told what happened to me on a medical level, even though I spent 10 days in the mental hospital so they had plenty of time to tell me! No-one kept me or my chap informed along the way as they promised. Anyway more about that later.

All I needed was sleep. Someone to say everything was going to be OK, to comfort me, give me a hug and soothe my racing mind. To tell me that I was safe. That life was safe. That nothing bad was happening. Sadly things had gone too far by this point which was what led to my sectioning which created a whole new level of fear!

I was literally out of the frying pan and into the fire!

BTW a few weeks prior to all of this kicking off I did my eleventh fire walk. Yes, one of those events where you walk on hot coals. It was the first charity fire walk I'd ever done. I am also trained in fire tending so I'm certainly not a girl who's scared of a bit of fire but this situation and what followed was a whole new level of burning in the fires of life!

I feel I have to back up to a few days before my 'weekend from hell' as there was some alcohol involved. I said I would keep it real. After all the stress of what happened, I turned to a few glasses of wine (well maybe a bottle! & then a few beers mixed in for good measure).

Being honest, I had also been drinking every night that week to try and help me cope with what was happening and also to maybe induce some kind of drink fuelled super sleep. Nope. That didn't work very well either and obviously just compounded the feelings of panic and fear.

Alcohol. A poison in itself!

Added to the toxic environment I had been involved in during the lead up to my breakdown things were going from bad to worse.

An old cycle of mine when I was growing up, (do we ever re-

ally grow up?) was to drink far too much then cry lots and either phone friends or go off looking for help and support with
whatever I was dealing with at the time. I went knocking on our
friends' door at midnight on one of the evenings the week before
my breakdown, but they didn't answer as they were in bed, so I
called my spiritual friend. My chap was running down the street
after me trying to contain me. Throughout this process really old
patterns, habits and cycles were coming up for recycling. It's fas-
cinating to look back but also brings up lots of sadness.

My tear ducts are still healing from all of the crying I did throughout this process and thank goodness my sense of humour is starting to return (only just! but PHEW!). I'm still fresh from 'The
Ward' as I share this story with you. It's only a short time since
my release, I know that time heals and already by sharing this
here with you I am starting to feel the headaches, tensions and
stresses lift a little. On a lighter note I've detoxed myself, lost lots
of weight and feel much more in control of my life, not that any
of us are really ever 'in control'.

So yes, the weekend from hell was born from a week of nightmarish goings on, very little if any proper sleep, alcohol, lack of
routine, food, water and all those good things both us and plants
require to grow or at least survive!

It's interesting that I remember almost everything that went on,
in detail too. I guess that's how writing this book will help to heal,
to release what's in my head. I have a strong memory too which

isn't always a great thing to have when you've been involved in something like this... or is it?

At this point I also have to give a HUGE shout out to my close friends and of course my chap and my mum and dad. We live in an outstanding rural village in Yorkshire not too far from the Peak District. My weekend from hell was made better by those close by. Who knows what would have happened if I lived alone or in a city, all those bright lights aren't for me. They also helped me to cut down on the alcohol and reminded me this wouldn't help. On the Sunday when the police came for me I was certain they assumed I was pissed as a fart but I wasn't. More to come on that!

Chapter 2

The Weekend From Hell

It started on the Friday, I was calling people, reaching out and letting them know what had happened, saying we needed support as we were tired. My dog needed walking, I didn't feel confident enough to even take him out, our friends helped us, we had offers of support but I don't think anyone realised how bad things had got at this point. My chap seemed annoyed that I had been calling for support, I felt like I had done the wrong thing but I knew he was absolutely knackered too and I felt scared to be on my own when he went to work.

One of my friends from the village came over to see me, I made us a cup of tea, my dog was playing up so I asked if we could go upstairs so I could lie down on the bed. Once again I relayed everything which had happened in the past few weeks, I also went through all of the messages, texts and calls again, trying to understand what had happened and why things got so bad. I knew I needed to sleep but no matter what I did I could not switch off or relax.

I also spoke regularly with one of my other close friends, she tried to help me the best she could, I kept asking her to take my phone off me. The weekend prior I had broken down at her house when everything was kicking off, even at that point I felt helpless.

I remember thinking I have to do something. I don't feel right, this isn't normal. I needed to speak to someone, get some help ASAP. I even called a well known mental health charity to get some counselling. They told me there was a two month waiting list or I could upgrade and be seen within two weeks if I paid £200. This confused me as I thought they were a charity and I didn't have this kind of money to spend on support.

I had also put a brief post online about what had happened on Friday 13th, I couldn't say much but I think most people sensed my unrest. I had lots of comments and a few phone calls too.

I could feel everything building up, it was as if I couldn't move through any of the feelings and emotions which were happening on the inside, even though on the outside I was sharing how I was feeling.

I also had a few conversations with some of the other people involved in the sectioning of our friend on that day too. Things had gone from bad to worse, it upset me so much, a couple of the others involved even joked it might be me next!

I sent out copies of all the messages to various people on the Friday, in case anything bad happened at the hospital with my

---

friend. I started to imagine there might be a stabbing or some kind of attack. I wasn't certain this nightmare was over and it wasn't, it was my turn next!

Over the course of the weekend the lovely little village in which we live became very, very scary. Some of this was thanks to the internet, news, media, what I experienced the week before and my now overactive imagination trying to make sense of everything. As well as many other things I'd picked up collected and stored in my clever brain muscle for the last 40 years!

On a side note (oops! I'd better be careful here as the internet said people with mental issues often digress or go off on tangents), I love emojis and I love gifs (that's gifs online not gifts although I love those too!) At this point I had started doing emoji faces and acting out my own gifs, like the one of the exploding head and the one of the OMG did that really just happen face! The fear though. The fear was underlying it all.... I felt I could no longer express myself as no-one understood.

We had some very strange and scary things which happened to me and my chap that weekend too, and these things REALLY did happen. We were in two near miss car accidents. We had a very freaky 'coincidence' related to the 9/11 terrorist attacks. We saw tiny baby lambs wearing raincoats (yes that really happens in the countryside apparently) and watched some odd stuff on the telly too! We had massive unexplainable synchronicities and lots of humming the Close Encounters of the Third Kind theme tune moments, it was very trippy!

I am a big believer in synchronicity, serendipity and what I like to call everyday magic. Right place right time and wrong place wrong time kind of stuff. I still hold my belief that everything happens for a reason and even though everything may not always feel magical it'll be OK. In the end it was just about OK, otherwise I wouldn't be here sharing my story but let's be blunt it was a very fucked up journey along the way and I have been left feeling like my life has fallen apart. It's going to take some time to put it back together again.

Part 1 - Saturday

What follows is somewhere between actual reality and what I imagined to be real and shows you how things can be misinterpreted and misunderstood when in psychosis.

For me even the bits which may not have been real felt very real, it was the reality I now found myself in. I was beyond scared.

Our dog poo police in the village became enforcers of an imaginary curfew I had conjured up after seeing some online articles which came up when I googled knife crimes and our local village. At the time gangs of youths were targeting each other in big cities but in my head they were here and on my doorstep with their guns and knives.

What once used to be a lovely peaceful evening stroll up the lane with our labradoodle dog Milo became a survival mission in which my chap had to accompany me everywhere for safety's sake as we were out after curfew.

It was also the weekend of the Syrian bombings so part of me thought that bombs would be going off and that we had new rules and rulers to follow. Women had to be with men at all times and any women without a partner (male) or any children or animals to care for were being targeted and executed. I had to make sure I was being subservient and following the rules.

Internet stuff really didn't help me at this point as lots of people were posting pictures of themselves with their 'man' that day too and my chap didn't like his picture posting online so I couldn't prove my relationship to the imaginary people I thought were going to kill us.

This particular weekend we had also arranged to feed a few neighbours cats and walk a friend's dog so we had stuff to do, regardless of the lack of sleep. Plus my chap had to work to try and catch-up what he'd missed during the manic week before. It was all too much. Lots of stuff to sort and no way out.

I felt very overwhelmed.

All I could do was ride the wave.

This wave my mind was creating, which I believed was actual reality! It wasn't all bad as some of my states were quite high, I felt

I was psychic and had a new level of consciousness but the under-lying current behind mostly everything I was doing was fear. Fear for my life and the lives of all of those around me. Not just the ones I knew but EVERYONE! The world! The whole planet! WE WERE NOT SAFE!

I was flitting between all kinds of stories. I see that now, they were just stories. Old stuff regurgitated, recent stuff retold and rewired in my broken brain, simply trying to figure out how to survive this horrific experience.

As I mentioned the internet and TV didn't help either, including the build-up to this happening. I've never been one for watching the news or reading the newspapers as I feel a lot of it is sensationalised and usually mostly the bad news which is shared. Once again I kept seeing updates online so had an idea of what was happening in the world but it was completely blown out of proportion in my head.

We also live on the Trans Pennine Trail so lots of people with backpacks were walking past my cottage on that Saturday, I must admit it was unusually busy which didn't help either and with the previous 9/11 connection I mentioned earlier I thought they all had bombs in their backpacks too!

It seemed that wherever we went everyone was rushing about, things appeared to be playing on fast forward. When out and about I saw a few people I know and had brief chats about what had happened the week before and how scared I had been and how tired I was.

I found that once I started to talk about what happened others opened up and shared their experiences of loss or times in their lives when they had had some kind of difficult situation to deal with, joining together in the pains of life so to speak. For me I was wide open energetically taking everything onboard. I had also started to cry a lot!

What on earth was happening?

How were we going to survive?

Before the weekend from hell, some months previously, I had decided to create an online group called 'Safety in Numbers Sisterhood' after I had an encounter with a strange guy in the local countryside. Maybe he was simply hitting on me but it didn't feel right so I ended up sharing this online and going live on one of my walks for moral support from other like-minded women.

After my breakdown I cleared, cancelled and deleted this group as well as some of the other things I was involved in online. I cleared away anything which felt like it was draining my energy or giving me some kind of responsibility for others. The ironic thing is the week prior when I actually felt extremely unsafe the last thing on my mind was to do a live video!

Anyway, the reason I mention said group was to say that a few

THE DAY I GOT SECTIONED

weeks prior someone had posted a police safety video called 'Tell, Run, Hide!' It was all about knife and gun crime and said the threat to the UK is severe and imminent and what we should do in a life threatening situation like this. I hadn't watched it up until the weekend from hell so as you can imagine this added to confirming my nightmares were coming true!

I understand stuff like this can be useful, I also understand that sadly people are involved in serious crimes but is it appropriate that any of us have access to these kind of videos at any time? Or to have the plethora of internet bombardment about crime and all of the terrible things happening in the world?

I feel we should have more say over this. We should have more choice about what flashes up on news feeds and in related posts online.

My fear flames were being well and truly fanned!

We did what needed to be done on the Saturday morning, I had also text another of my friends in the village who said I could pop up for a chat, my chap dropped me off as he took Milo, our dog for a walk, I collapsed in her doorway with my wellies on crying. She scooped me up and made cups of tea. We sat and chatted and ate crisps, I told her everything which had happened the week prior, not realising I was sinking deeper and deeper the more I spoke, everything felt so surreal, I felt highly sensitive and psychic again but at least I felt we had some more support. I spoke to her chap too as he has had past experience with mental health issues so this helped me to understand a little more. We ate some sandwiches when my chap came back with Milo, we did our best to laugh things off and be normal. A little squirrel came to the window, it looked like it waved at us. We went on our way with hugs and thank yous as I cautiously walked back to our house trying to appear normal.

We fed the cats and walked the dogs which was really hard and confusing. I had to get bathed twice this day as I was so hot and sweaty. The new boiler didn't have a digital clock so it ticked really loudly. Each time I got a bath or freshened myself up in the bathroom I thought it was a ticking bomb. I couldn't relax. Our old enamelled bath had also been accidentally scratched whilst the boiler was being fitted, to me it looked like a witch had run her nails across it which scared me too. We had bought a little pot of enamel paint which was like tippex, every time we painted over the scratches it peeled off and they came back again! Even a bath didn't relax me and being out and about tipped me over another edge.

The world was moving so fast and so was everyone in it. I could feel the world rotating and spinning, I was struggling to stay in balance. We saw people we know in the village and I tried to assess if they looked safe and if they were OK without saying too much or appearing too weird.

Act normal Liz!

Saturday afternoon meant a trip out to get some food supplies so we chose to go to our local farm shop and keep it simple. This meant driving past the house I'd spent time at the previous week which also gave me the heebie jeebies. Once we arrived at the farm shop it was absolutely packed as there was some kind of horse show on and people everywhere. I daren't get out of the car, I didn't feel safe. I wasn't convinced my chap was safe either, I remember sitting in the car with the windows down frantically watching for him coming out.

When he appeared I dragged him into the car, saying "lock the doors, close the windows we aren't safe!!!"

At this point I had all the previous fears stacking up as well as the amount of horses about too. My dog Milo is scared of horses so he starts barking and rearing up if he sees one. Where we live is also a favourite with horse riders and usually I love to see them riding past my house but on this particular day I wondered if women on horses were taking over the world too!

Once again this was harking back to what I had experienced the previous week and what felt unsafe or unsupported.

I remember seeing two ladies confidently riding past our cottage when we got home wondering if they were actually the new 'law enforcement' trying to keep us safe. What the hell was happening?

The journey home was frantic, it was at this point we had one of our near miss car accidents too. Usually after something like this I would be relieved to get back to my lovely little cottage. I did feel a slight inkling of relief but then the living nightmares started again.

I couldn't settle. How could anyone? Something really bad was about to happen or so I believed.

I also weaved in a storyline about all the local farmers trying to take over and men were taking over the world. You see there's also a lot of tractors and traditional Yorkshire blokes go up and down our lane, plus a number of vans and workmen. It's not out of the ordinary to see an old steam engine tractor passing by or an old vintage Land Rover or car. This too became another one of my triggers.

I was so confused! What year was it again?

We also have a local hunt each year and lots of shooting (which I don't personally agree with but it's local tradition), guns were going off in the distance, I remember thinking "this is it, Armageddon is here we are all goners!"

In between all of this someone had been photographing our cottage that morning. I told my chap and he thought it was my overactive imagination again. I actually found out later (once I was released and back home) that it was a builder for my lovely neighbour next door photographing our porch as she's having one built too.

Lots of stuff that appeared to be happening to make me even more scared did have explanations but nonetheless it was way too much to take!

THEY ARE WATCHING US!

WE AREN'T SAFE!

YOU AREN'T SAFE!

THE WORLD'S NOT SAFE!

WE ARE GOING TO DIE!

Or was I already dead?

HELP!!!!

We watched a bit of TV that afternoon but I imagined the programmes were about our local area. In my head they were showing where people had been killed and what atrocities had happened. I also imagined there were lots of religious programmes on trying to form some kind of worldwide cult or brainwash everyone into believing what the bible says. On the Saturday evening we decided to watch a film. Films have always been our thing, I've been known in the past to say that life's like a movie and that we create our own story lines.

Not sure where this horror film I was starring in got created! Please can I have a retake?

At this point I was under the impression that I could only move around the house or help my chap at designated times in case anyone saw me in front of a window and I would be shot.

We had to look happy and pretend everything was OK so as not to alert anyone in the village that something was wrong. Everytime someone passed our front window I smiled and laughed, I was really starting to freak my chap out!

Recently we also had a fabulous wooden sign put up on the grass triangle near our cottage all about the history of our village, it even spoke about the witches who used to live here and their dreadful fate back in the 1600s.

Was this a modern version of said Witch Trial?

Was this because I liked magic?

Was it because I have a sign outside my door that says 'Be Nice Or Leave'? (I really do have that sign BTW)

Had I done something wrong?

We watched the film Wonder with Julia Roberts, I intend to watch it again with my mind back to normal but at the time it felt like a very confusing film, my sensations were heightened and I could see hidden messages in the film. More and more overwhelment, confusion and uncertainty about life and don't get my started on Britain's Got Talent! OMG BGT!

Now that really tipped me over the edge on the Saturday evening. There was a guy on there who also lived 'Up North', not too far away from us doing an escape artist trick, Ant or Dec had to help him escape by choosing the correct keys. I was also conscious that Ant was going through his own issues with mental health from what I had seen online and in my head the guy died! Then at some point later in the evening, when it was dark, I imagined he was the 'Doctor Death' guy that the medical doctor had spoken of a few days earlier. I thought he was coming to kill us!

I also imagined a guy who once cyber flashed me was attempting to shoot us if we stood too close to any windows as well as everything else! He was a conspiracy theorist and felt very unsafe on the one short occasion I met him.

I know it's a lot to take in.

It was for me too!

I probably haven't even covered it all here and we haven't even got to the Police, the Ambulance, Casualty or The Ward yet. It was scary as hell!

Back to BGT, it was a very manic programme that evening with longer than usual pauses and some strange acts from around the world even though it's about British talent. I have to add at this point too that I have never and will never be racist in any way, I do my best to be politically correct and wouldn't ever want to offend. Each to their own. It's all good. I am just saying it all added to my confusion at the time.

There were lots of people from different countries, ethnicities and backgrounds all showcasing their talents. In my state of mind watching this from a place of fear and panic it felt as if some kind of crime was going to happen live on TV! There was also a group of singers raising awareness of giving blood, I thought they were on there due to all the stabbings and crime as we were short of blood to help save people. With my upbringing as a Jehovah's Witness the blood thing has always been an uncomfortable one for me, at this point I thought we needed to give blood as soon as possible too!

During one of the other 'strange' acts we had a power cut at which point I thought the TV had been cut because of a bombing live on TV, I've never held my chaps hand so tight. This is it I thought!

We are goners...... We are all doomed!

Then the power came back on.

Things were getting stranger and stranger.

I also noticed there were a lot of odd programmes on TV when we flicked between the channels which brought up more uncomfortable stuff.

At one point I decided I wanted to watch the news as things appeared to be completely out of control and I wanted to make sure we were safe, my chap said it wasn't the best thing for me to be watching in my state.

I kept asking again and again "Are we safe?" "Are you safe?" "Is the world safe?"

I have some relatives who live aboard I was very worried about them too. My uncle, my brother, had they died too?

Then comes the really freaky bit!

At one point I actually thought I had died. I thought I had been stabbed and I was the spirit (ghost) of myself wandering around aimlessly between worlds. My chap was so tired at this point he wasn't answering me or speaking to me all of the time, he was totally overwhelmed with it all too and I was talking constantly.

This led me to wondering if he had died and I was seeing his spirit (ghost), a few weeks earlier he had been to a gig at the MEN Arena Manchester where the bombings happened a year before.

This was a very eerie feeling. I've never felt so close to death. I recounted the last few weeks to try and piece everything together.

I was questioning everything and most of all everyone's safety.

Running around like a crazy woman trying to keep us all safe. I didn't know what to do!

That night I didn't sleep again.

I remember holding my chap so tightly, hugging him harder than ever before I bet we looked like the old couple in the film Titanic just before the ship sinks! That's how I felt. Hold on for dear life, make sure you tell everyone you love them!

THIS IS IT LIZ!

I've never sweat so much in my life! I was up in the early hours running another bath. I needed to be as normal as possible, act normal, stay safe.

But that just wasn't possible.

Part 2 - Sunday

On the Sunday morning I decided to choose to wear a pair of jeans and a new top I hadn't worn before. The top had butterflies all over it so I thought this would make me feel better and also appear more normal. I put my make-up on, washed my hair, extra deodorant as the sweat was pouring off me at this point.

Act normal Liz. Be as normal as you can.

What's normal again?

Where's that box I need to fit into?

I've always been unique and let my crazy flag fly a fair bit in my life. One of my favourite poems being the 'Crazy Ones' 293from the old Apple advert. I would say I am a slightly crazy sane woman. BTW I've never been diagnosed with any mental health issues, I am a bit 'Ipso Facto' as my chap calls it and am a very emotional person but this was way beyond any normal I was used to! BTW 'Ipso Facto' is another film connection, it's the words of a song from About a Boy with Hugh Grant. It's taken from the scene where the lovely hippy lady cries over the cornflakes every morning. I wasn't quite that bad before all of this but have always been a big believer in allowing our emotions to come up and out.

Better out than in!

Emotions actually means energy in motion.....

My energies were in way too much motion by this point, I couldn't stop what was happening!

Inside I was dying, literally. What the fuck was going off? Why was all this scary stuff happening? How were we going to survive?

My chap was up early to watch the Grand Prix, I'm not a fan of motor sports and never watch it with him but on this particular morning I thought I had to be with him as much as I could to save us. I managed to make a little discombobulated breakfast, no beans or mushrooms today as I didn't want to use a sharp knife. I felt sick when I tried to eat, the racing cars whizzing about on the TV.

I asked a few questions about the race to try and calm the racing of my own mind but felt paranoid as I knew I was acting really odd. The race happened to be in the country where my brother was living and due to the dramatic camera work and lots of people in the crowds on their phones I thought a bomb was or had gone off there too, I thought my brother was dead or in danger too!

At this point I was turning my phone off and hiding it away in various drawers around the house as it was all too much, I kept forgetting where I had put it and flitted between needing my phone and hating my phone with all of its connectivity to the world. Each time I reunited with my phone I checked Facebook for those updates people create when disasters happen, I was checking to see if people I knew had marked themselves safe but I couldn't get any confirmation.

At the end of the race the winner was spraying a huge giant bottle of champagne all over the place, then he poured it into his sweaty shoe and drank from it, he also offered it around to everyone else.

The world had gone mad!

I asked my chap if that was really happening, he said this particular driver always does that if he wins. I wondered if they were doing all this to distract everyone from what was really happening in the world. It was really fucking odd. I knew we needed to go out again soon too and was feeling well freaked out!

My brain did not get what was happening whether real or imagined or blown out of proportion.

We went on the cat feeding run. BTW my chap's nickname is Cat which created some funny confusion with people who didn't know this. I was going to feed the cats with my Cat. Was I now the crazy cat lady?

No-one was understanding me.

We nipped in and out of the neighbours houses. I was constantly checking we were safe.

At this point a trip down to the local shop completely freaked me out let alone a full blown dog walk.

I chose a simple walk which is connected with some amazing local history about witches (maybe not the best choice) Cuckstool Road where they used to dip the witches in the water to see if they sank or swam, the cuckstool is the seat they used to sit the witches on.

As I've briefly mentioned before I have been known to dabble in a bit of magic myself from time to time. For me magic is more about day to day life being magical but during the previous few months I'd opened up to more alternative ways of living which had also stuck with me.

Over the course of the last year or so I had also been known to call myself a witch, which actually means wise woman.

I wasn't feeling very wise right now and truly felt that no amount of magic could help me. Were some old spirits being stirred up?

Had I been cursed?

Last time I delved into 'witchy stuff' I got the end of my thumb bitten off by a dog. (That actually happened! About five years earlier).

This felt way more serious!

We walked the path and I tried to breathe as deeply as I could. Breathe in. Breathe out.

Maybe I am going to die because I am a witch?

Maybe this actually was a modern day Witch Trial?

Or maybe I have been hypnotised or possessed like I was told I would as a child if I delved into anything too out of the ordinary.

It was all coming up and out.

We didn't see many people on the walk but I remember some cyclists going past, quite a large group of guys on mountain bikes, I put my head down and made sure I didn't make eye contact, I held my chap's arm and did my best to look subservient.

On the Sunday afternoon my chap took me to my mum and dad's. This was after a few times running up and down our street to alert my neighbours and friends about being unsafe as well as asking for their help.

The weather was also really strange this weekend too, sometimes it was thick fog other times the sun came out and it was red hot. The fog scared me, I didn't want to go out in the car again, what if something happened?

Before we were due to leave I thought there was someone with a knife in my loft, I tried to get my friends to help us check the house. I was running up and down the street in a panic, I didn't know what to do. At this point they looked really worried too so I took this to mean that all the stuff I was experiencing was real.

I was also starting to confuse what I was seeing and wondered if everyone was staring at me because I'd won the lottery the night before, is that why someone was taking pictures outside my window? Or had my friends won the lottery, they looked really posh today, were they going to collect their winnings?

I was flitting between the worse and best scenarios, I guess this was part of my coping mechanism.

I kept being told that things would be better once I had been to mum and dad's. That I was going to be OK, that I needed some sleep, some help and some support.

Driving to my mum and dad's freaked me out as by this point I also thought that the local gun and knife wielding youths were on the loose again and it was foggy and grey, no sunshine and no blue skies, the world felt dismal. At least my chap promised to drive a little bit slower by this point which helped.

I thought my head was about to explode. Cue head explosion gif or emoji!

To be serious though, by this point I daren't even joke about anything. What I did decide to do on the drive over was go with the lottery win scenario as it felt lighter than the one where we all die.

I also decided that the kids and teenagers were going to do well at running the world as people much younger than me created lots of the magical stuff I enjoyed online like Facebook.

I was still scared at this point but managed to contain my fear and trust that it'd be ok once we got to mum and dad's. The motorway was ridiculous so I closed my eyes which made me feel sick, at least we only had one junction to go and mum and dad aren't too far away.

My mum and dad are outstanding people, but they had no idea what had been happening. Same goes for my chap throughout this process, our love is stronger then ever, he did his best too as did my close friends. They are all outstanding people who did what they could.

We all did. Everyone was doing their best.

We are perfectly imperfect.

Imperfect = I'm~Perfect.

I had a wonderful catch-up with another dear friend who supported me though this, we met up again after my release and we had some giggles about organising an 'outstanding people party' for all involved! Maybe later.

Unfortunately when we arrived at mum and dad's there were two young lads out back playing football. I imagined one of them had a disfigured face like the little boy in the film we had watched the night before. I managed to smile say hi and quickly walk past before they did anything to me, Milo my dog or my chap. I was on the edge of a ledge.

Even more unfortunately we opened the door to my dad in the kitchen making a buttie. He loves cooking and is usually found making some kind of delicious food. But on this day he had a huge bread knife in his hand. HELP!

Major trigger button pressed! I ran over to him saying "dad you aren't safe! Put the knife down! We aren't safe!"

What unfolded both breaks my heart and makes me feel a lot of self-judgment and shame. I know it's healing with time and I am eternally grateful for all of the support and everyone's way of dealing with what happened.

Chapter 3

The Damage Was Done

I kept flitting back to the possible lottery win scenario as this brought a bit of welcome relief. I wondered if they were waiting until I had calmed down to tell me about our millions as it was a big deal. Could this be what's happening? Something amazing rather than something awful?

BTW I've never been big into the lottery and you will often hear me saying we create our own magic with money via our own unique skills and talents but at this point I was open to anything. I've always worried about money since I was a small girl.

I also started to wonder if something had happened to my mum and dad. Were they well? Were they safe? It feels awful to type this here but I also thought one of them may have dementia and feared greatly for their wellbeing.

The Facebook stuff started to come back at this point too and rather than me posting a picture of a pink fluffy love heart online with a lovely pic of me with my mum or dad I started shouting out "I LOVE MY MUM SHE HAS DEMENTIA" or "I LOVE MY DAD HE HAS DEMENTIA".

Bless them!

Bless me!

Bless my chap witnessing this unravelling!

Obviously they wanted me to be quiet and were scared too, I was out of control. In my head I thought if I kept shouting these things out then 'The Kids' who had taken over the world wouldn't kill us. I also started to wonder if we were in some kind of surreal game show setting where at the end of all of this madness I would win a prize for my honesty. Oh dear. Not the case. As I said before hindsight is a powerful thing but by this point I was too far gone. There was no game show, there were no winnings, just madness!

There was an amount of time where me and my mum chatted calmly as I tried to keep her safe and well, we had pens and a Zen colouring book, all was well for a little while. I thought I was helping her.

In fact she was trying to help me.

So was my dad and my chap.

They knew I needed to sleep. Sleep would heal. I was far from any form of sleep or rest.

We also spent a while writing messages on a chalk board I had taken with me. One of those little chalk boards you put in your kitchen to write notes on. I started to use it to try and communicate with them. Scratching out chalk messages so as not to have to shout. I was also getting everyone to try and lip-read me so I could be calm and quiet.

At this point I had also decided that my chap had to marry me in order for us to either survive or win the lottery. Lots of old stuff was coming up about my upbringing and religious stuff which again felt very unsafe in my world as it now was. I also admitted to my parents that the year before, whilst smoking a little medicinal marijuana, I had decided to burn my bible to free myself of religion. During this little escapade I found out that bibles are printed on paper that doesn't like to burn! Who would have thought it!

It took me three hours to burn 'the good book', at one point pages were floating up and out of my chimney, I was worried the neighbours would see them. I'm a rebellious soul, I can't help it! That said it made me feel like I had committed major sins.

Had I done something wrong?

Was Armageddon here?

Was the world going to end?

At one point I said my brother and his wife had been bombed. I remember saying to my mum and dad they needed to know that he was gone. Looking back now it was so sad and also so mad!

Madness. Crazy time. WTF was going on?!?!

There was no stopping me.

I was totally confused and bewildered by it all.

What was the truth?

What was reality and what was not?

In amongst all of this I remember my dad trying to get me to go upstairs and sleep. There were scissors upstairs and they scared me too. Not because I was going to use them, because I didn't think anyone was safe around anything sharp.

Throughout this process I wasn't violent, the worst I did was throw a few cups of water at people I deemed to be unsafe and some very tight handholding of those who felt safe. Earth angels who would help me get through this.

Yes there was a lot of shouting and commotion. At one point I was dancing and Milo my dog was jumping up at me, humping me, like dogs do!

I remember being 'told off' for this.

CALM DOWN LIZ!

BE QUIET!

Shoe on the other foot I would have been saying the same but I was trying to express myself and let all of this energy up and out!

Milo needed to go walkies so my dad took him. Again I was up, I was shouting "he isn't safe, my dad's not safe, Milo isn't safe. Milo might bite someone, they may get hurt, something bad is going to happen!"

SOMEONE HELP ME!

NO-ONE IS SAFE!

It seemed to go on for hours, which it did, we'd missed our Sunday dinner but food was the last thing on my mind.

Gently does it. She needs sleep.

I was saying totally out there stuff shouting and releasing. Years and years of layers unfolding and stuff which happened throughout my life coming up and out in the open.

I had no filter.

Eventually my chap had to call 111 to try and get some help, he asked if I could get some sleeping tablets but as it was Sunday there were no doctors. They said we could go to a drop in place behind the shopping centre in a local city centre.

When he told me this I freaked as I thought that's where another bombing would happen. I also regurgitated stuff from years ago when I used to go to a local spiritual group behind the very same shopping centre with some really unique folk. Each to their own they were all good, I am into alternative stuff too but at this point the memories didn't serve me very well.

I refused to go.

It wasn't safe for me, him or anyone else and I certainly couldn't get back in the car let alone go to a big city!

The thing is I've never really liked big cities or busy places let alone in this state. Plus it was Sunday evening by now and all the pissheads would be out too.

I was beyond overwhelmed!

Things were escalating!

What was I going to do?

My chap called 111 back to ask if a doctor could come out as I was too afraid to go into the city centre.

No-one was available.

There was no help.

I was shouting in the background trying to say "WE AREN'T SAFE! I CAN'T GO THERE! HELP ME! WE ARE ALL GOING TO DIE" I was even trying to grab the phone to let them know terrifying things were happening in the world and there was no way I was going there.

Because I was kicking up a fuss and they couldn't hear what I was saying they told my chap it would have to be escalated. The 111 people called the police. Funnily enough 111 has always been a magical number of mine, it didn't feel very magical anymore that's for sure!

It only took them about five minutes to arrive. Ironic that it took an hour for them to get to my friend a few days earlier when she needed their support urgently.

It was like the comedy of errors, so was the mental hospital and we haven't even got there yet! Believe you me there was absolutely no laughter involved in all of this process! Just lots and lots of sadness, fear, worry and me being completely out there!

Two police cars, an ambulance, flashing lights and some very fierce looking men later I was feeling even more out of control.

Big burly men in their full police gear was not what I needed right now, but this is how the system is set up, there is no middle ground. There is no loving support or healing retreat and there definitely wasn't any hugs going round at this point.

Fortunately there were two female police officers so I said I didn't want any men near me and asked to stay with the police women in the lounge.

One of them looked a little like my spiritual friend who had been supporting me through the previous week's nightmare, I asked her if she was an angel. She said she could be an angel if I wanted her to be.

I looked into her eyes to check if I trusted her. I have always felt that you can connect with the truth of people by their eyes, I am intuitive and get a really good sense of people quite quickly. She was safe but I'm not sure if her hands were as I was holding them so very tightly.

I asked her name but couldn't focus on what she was saying so decided to call her by my spiritual friend's name. I chose to call the other police woman by another name too, I was having to do whatever made me feel just a little bit more relaxed.

They asked me about my colouring in, things felt a little calmer for a small period of time but I could see the policemen kept wanting to come into the lounge and that was making me feel very edgy.

In the background one of the policemen had told my chap that this wasn't going to be pretty and that they had to get me out of the house and into the ambulance. Some of the next bit is a blur as it all seemed to happen really fast.

I was trying my best to determine who was the safest to be with. In normal circumstances, mainly because of the Meniere's disease and my past experiences with vertigo and blackouts, I always like to have a plan and know people I'm travelling with in case anything happens to my health.

I spotted a kind looking policeman who looked quite young and seemed energetically softer than the other bruisers! There was also another policeman who seemed less intense than the others. They said they would go with me as well as the two female officers.

One of the very tall strong looking policemen barged into the room, he really scared me so I shouted "YOU ARE NOT SAFE!!" and threw my cup of water over him, that's when things escalated.

I ran to the stairs, my dad was trying to grab me, all kinds of awful stuff was happening in my head, he fell over and landed on top of me, the police had to think about his safety as well and moved him away.

They grabbed my arms and dragged me outside up the stone steps, I remember thinking my feet were being broken as they smashed into the cold hard concrete.

I managed to become free from their grip and nearly ran out into the road, I could see them stopping the cars in the distance as it's quite a busy road where my mum and dad live.

I will still shouting out various things at this point.

I can be known to be a bit of a joker and bit risqué or cheeky and it was during this part of the journey that side of me started to emerge.

The thing is, I was absolutely fucking terrified.

I was already terrified over the course of the days leading up to this.

I didn't think I could be any more scared.

They got me into the ambulance as I tried to assess if the ambulance man was a good guy or a bad guy, he looked like one of the farmers in our village as he was wearing green overalls, he didn't feel safe!

The kind looking policeman had come with me into the ambulance along with the female officers so I held his hand as tightly as I could staring into his eyes and asking him if we were safe.

My coping mechanism of humour was coming out in full swing now as I started to shout "PINK FLUFFY LOVE HEARTS" as loud as I possibly could asking him to do his best 'Peaky Blinders' impression.

On a side note if you haven't seen Peaky Blinders watch it. I have a crush on one of the characters Tommy Shelby (I don't think I'm the only one!) and love all of the horses and strong women featured in that programme. It's based on a true life story about a group of gangsters.

Now it was manifesting as a way of winning the imaginary competition. If I got someone to do a Peaky Blinders brummy Tommy impression I would be saved! I would win!

Obviously that was NOT the case.

To my dismay he kept saying "Sorry love I can't do a Peaky Blinders impression" I'm sure he had a slight grin on his face at one point but maybe that was my imagination too?

I was so sacred he would let go of my hand and each time the ambulance stopped I thought I had to shout random stuff out so 'The Kids' wouldn't kill us.

"I LOVE MY MUM SHE'S GOT DEMENTIA!"

"I LOVE MY DAD HE'S GOT DEMENTIA!"

"PINK FLUFFY LOVE HEARTS!"

All of this stuff was coming up from what I had experienced before all this shit hit the proverbial fan.

When I got scared I started shouting out "I HAVE SEPSIS I'M GOING TO DIE".

Time seemed to morph at this stage. We arrived at the hospital and as I got out of the ambulance I jumped up at the kind young policeman arms and legs akimbo and wrapped myself around him like one of those cheeky little monkeys at the zoo, I was begging him to do his 'Tommy' impression.

"No love, sorry I can't do that!!!"

I felt scared, ashamed, embarrassed, daft, silly, stupid, wrong, useless, funny, cheeky, lost, confused and fearful all at the same time.

I remember being wheeled into the hospital room shouting "I HAVE SEPSIS! I HAVE SEPSIS!" and being hushed and shushed.

Was this why I felt this way? Did I have blood poisoning? Nope. That wasn't it!

The tiny and very warm room was in the centre of two very busy corridors, it was only small but had two sets of doors. It was like an office from the 80s. Even more people kept coming and going.

Could this day get any more manic?

"I LOVE MY MUM SHE'S GOT DEMENTIA!"

"I LOVE MY DAD HE'S GOT DEMENTIA!"

"PINK FLUFFY LOVE HEARTS!"

More people staring at me.

More people coming and going.

By this point my mum made an announcement in the waiting room to say "I AM LIZ'S MUM & I DO NOT HAVE DEMENTIA!!"

Who were all of these people?

"YOU'RE NOT SAFE!"

"I'M NOT SAFE!"

"AM I SAFE? ARE YOU SAFE?"

My brain was completely gone by now. There were too many people, too many safety checks to do. I started to wonder if it was time for me to just give up and die, I could have been dead at this point anyway so it wouldn't have made much difference in my less than expert opinion.

I started to determine who was allowed in and out of the room and who must stay with me to keep me safe.

The earth angel policewoman sat next to me and let me squeeze her hand some more, she suggested meditation and asked what would help me calm down. I was confused but we did a little breathing together. I kept asking her what all the devices were on her police vest, they were buzzing and flashing all of the time which was overwhelming me too!

I wondered if she actually was an angel and this was the gates of heaven or hell.

Someone brought me a cup of water. I didn't want to throw this one on anyone I was spitting feathers thirsty with all of the shouting and trying to keep safe!

More Peaky Blinders stuff was happening as I thought they were bringing me gin! My chap designs T-shirts and a few months earlier he did a Peaky Blinders one for the gin Tommy had created. It said 'Gin, to help with incurable sadness'.

I'm pretty sure the police people thought I'd had a bottle or two of gin at this point anyway but the fact was I hadn't had any alcohol at all that day. The police asked me if I liked gin.

I kept drinking my gin water and tried to fathom out what I should do next.

The nice policeman disappeared at some point, when he came back he had taken his police vest off and unfortunately for him left his fly down! I asked why he looked different, he said he was warm so he'd taken his vest off. I looked down, he hadn't zipped up his fly! I shouted "You're flying low!! YOU'RE NOT SAFE!". He left the room, no more nice policeman for this crazy lady!

In between all of this I kept shouting stuff out like a jack in the box who wouldn't go away. Things kept popping out, I had no control over what I was doing and saying.

Bless my dad, he'd picked up my mum's slippers for me to wear but once again I thought this was his imaginary dementia as she's three sizes smaller than me so that felt strange.

The smallest things were triggering me into panic. As well as the HUGE things which had been happening around me.

Swirly whirly energy.

So many people.

So much overwhelment.

It was getting worse and worse.

Again I decided to go back to the game show storyline as this felt less stressful.

Before the police were called, to help me feel better, I'd decided that me, my chap and mum and dad would start doing high fives! Cheesy but true.

I was shouting out "Team Greenwood" high five or "Tommy wants a Snickers" high five (this was a different Tommy bTW not the Peaky Blinders one, this came from a joke we had with friends years and years ago!)

Like I said lots of stuff came up from my past most of it wasn't funny at all though. I am dealing with it and healing it! I'll get there!

Anyway, yes, lots and lots of people.

In and out, up and down.

Where was my chap? Was he still alive?

In reality he'd actually gone back home to drop Milo off and was coming straight back to the hospital but I thought otherwise. I thought I was in casualty. I wasn't sure though.

At some point someone mentioned the word upgrade, they were probably meaning I would be getting an upgrade out of this awful red hot sweaty little room into some kind of hospital bed but I thought they meant some kind of life upgrade.

Or should that be downgrade.

Were the people whom I said were safe going to be my new friends?

Was the nice policeman going to be my new chap?

Where were my friends?

Were women taking over the world?

Would there be any men anymore after all this?

Were men taking over the world?

Was I going to be forced to be a Jehovah's Witness to survive Armageddon?

Did I have to marry someone else?

So many scenarios so little time to process it all.

I'd started calling most of the other people by different names too but there were also synchronicities, my chap confirmed that actually some of the people did have the same names as people from my past which I had been talking about earlier. In reality some of the people did look like other people we knew. It was freaky! Maybe his lack of sleep too, who knows!

I had to keep checking people's name badges to see who they were to make sure they were safe. I also kept asking the police women why they had so many devices on their fluorescent yellow waistcoats as this felt very overwhelming too.

There were many hours spent toing and froing, trying to keep me calm, trying to stop me shouting and dancing. I wasn't one of those crazy people who takes all their clothes off and dances naked on a chair thank goodness. BTW no offence if you've ever done this as I know this can happen too, I did lift my top up at one point but knew from the look on everyone's faces that was not a good path to walk along right now! I jumped onto a chair at one point but through fear rather than to dance. I was shouting "GET BACK YOU ARE NOT SAFE!"

One of the nurses had kind eyes, she was an earth angel and I let her accompany me to the toilet as I hadn't peed for hours by this point, no I wasn't one of those crazy ones who pees themselves, well not at this point anyway. Believe it or not it gets A LOT WORSE and once again we haven't even got to the mental hospital yet!

I remember pointing all the poo stains on the toilet seat out to the nurse and trying to have a laugh with her saying how weird this all was, trying to fix my fears with humour again.

In the background my chap was back, he was explaining what had happened and all the stress and lack of sleep I had experienced, he even asked if they could just jab a needle in my arm and put me to sleep, don't worry not put me down, all I needed was sleep.

That protocol wasn't allowed, I had to be the one who made the wise decision to take the pill. Like I was in any state of mind to make that decision!

After dealing with disease in my life I am of the opinion that alternative therapies are totally amazing used in balance with medication when needed so I wasn't anti-medication I was simply trying to figure out what they were giving me and once again using film and TV as my guiding light. That wasn't made easy.

My mind was about to be blown on a new level!

I had to make the choice in my broken state!

WHO THE FUCK CHOSE TO MAKE THE PILL YOU HAVE TO TAKE BLUE!

Did the film The Matrix come before or after this decision?

They wanted me to take the little blue pill.

BOOM went my brain!

I couldn't remember which pill did what in the film The Matrix at this point, I needed to get my chap back in the room to help me decide.

He knew exactly what I was thinking, after 15 years together and about two-four films a week we have a lot of cinematic history together.

He said whichever pill they are giving me will help and to take the pill.

"But it's blue! What does the blue pill do in The Matrix? I can't remember".

I felt the panic rising in me again and some laughter too at being in such an absurd situation and this choice being so huge.

If I took the blue pill would I forever be stuck in a fake world? Where was the red pill?

Why didn't I have both choices.

I tried to hide it under my armpit but they saw me, so I decided to put the blue pill into my plastic cup of gin water which apparently renders it useless or possibly even bad to take once it's dissolved. I did change my mind a little later and was going to drink the blue pill water (which had a bit of fluff in it by this point too) everyone kept shouting "NO, DON'T TAKE IT!"

I was so very confused.

I wondered if there was some poo in the cup too?

They got me another blue pill but this time it came with two social workers. I didn't know they were social workers and in my head they were Jehovah's Witnesses coming to do an intervention because I had sinned (I'd heard this word in the hospital too and lots of the words during my upbringing were similar). Men in suits, smartly dressed men and women, bringing back old memories of my rebellion as a young teenager breaking free from the religious rules and regulations. The social worker guy didn't stand a chance as my dad kindly introduced him by name, his name matching up with some more bad memories I had regurgitated earlier in the day. His colleague was a kind looking lady who unfortunately looked like the woman who used to own our house. We'd seen her driving past a few days earlier.

"You used to live in my house!"

She looked at me like I'd lost it!

I had....

My chap knew what was going off, he tried to explain she looked like the lady who used to live in our house.

I looked at the social worker guy who seemed annoyed. Was he this particular man from my past, had he come to try and fix me or to take me away. What was he going to do?

He definitely wasn't safe in my eyes!

Once again it was system overload so I threw my cup of gin water in his face.

Bad move.

He was ushered out as I reassessed who was safe again and who wasn't, also was I being reprimanded for past wrongs and rules I hadn't followed?

Was I going to jail?

Guilt washed over me about all the things I have done in my life and how very wrong I was.

I still had the whole pill decision to make too.

From first hand experience it would really help if they made the pills pink or green, maybe even pink love heart shaped (or would this cost the pharmaceutical companies too much of their precious profits?). Tell you what just make this magical little pill white to save future confusion and please explain what it does to ease peoples decisions in the future!

There's even more stuff that happened but some of it blurs into the past now. I do remember having to have a 'meeting' with a medical person, along with two doctors who assessed me in my very broken state.

At this point I was going back to the week before and the reasons I had not slept I was trying to explain my actions but in a really messed up way. I was coming out with really odd stuff and messing up my words. I was way beyond it all, I was brimming over with the vastness of what had unfolded.

Out of the three people in that room assessing me I only felt semi-safe with one of them, the other two didn't say very much at all, I felt like they were looking at me like I was gone out, which I probably was.

The whole debacle went on for hours. I was exhausted and so was everyone else involved. The police left at some point.

I went to the toilet again, my dad accompanied me, I tried to jump up on him for a hug and hurt his knees. I felt really bad but I couldn't stop. I decided he had dementia again so I had to look after him, at least that took the pressure off me again for a while. My legs gave way a few times on the way to the toilet and I collapsed, my dad picked me up and dusted me off.

There were sick people everywhere trying to sleep. Was this the aftermath of the bombings? Was this what the world had come to?

We went back to the room with many doors and even more choices. Some more time passed.

Eventually, after lots more shouting, scared deliberation and precious time later.

I took the pill.

My dad prayed (bless him).

My mum looked relieved and gave me one of those amazing mother daughter I love you smiles.

CHAPTER 3

My chap looked absolutely exhausted (bless him).

And we all lived happily ever after.

NOT.

Behind the scenes the paperwork was signed in good faith to section me and give me the love, care and attention I so clearly needed. Everyone was assured that this would be best for me and all involved and that they would be involved in my healing process every step of the way.

That was clearly not the case!

Chapter 4

The Room Without A View

We were told they had found me a nice big room with plenty of space and its own toilet.

I was still worrying about what the blue pill did but no-one explained. I thought to myself well what's done is done now I will have to face the consequences of my actions.

The windows were covered in an opaque material so you couldn't see out. I could hear sirens all around me. The thoughts about the war and the bombings came back.

Then I wondered if each time someone left me they died. Was it my fault this was happening?

I climbed onto a very narrow metal bed, there were lots of chairs in the room too, those really awful blue plastic looking ones found in hospitals. It was all so clinical.

I laid down and crossed my hands over my chest like you would if you were in a coffin (well someone else would do this for you obviously).

I felt my chap's tears dripping on my face and I could vaguely see him standing over me crying. This is it I thought, judgment day!

He squeezed my hand before he had to leave, it was the early hours of the morning by now. He'd been told he had to go home and sleep otherwise he may end up getting sectioned with me. He was also sleep deprived and extremely stressed by this point.

Mum and dad stayed. There were no comforts for them either and they had to spend the next 12 hours sat on those awful blue chairs as if they needed all of this in their retirement years!

The moment when my chap left I thought he was gone forever. I was absolutely heartbroken. Everything went black.

I heard muffled voices, people coming in to check on me. Were they doing tests on me?

Was I being raped?

I sunk into a black hole of nothingness.

The next morning arrived. I woke up very scared.

Lots of sadness and tears and lots of questions.

I thought I had made the wrong choice.

I thought my chap was dead (again).

I wondered if I was dead (again).

I thought I was being taken to a new reality. Not the upgrade you would hope, wish and dream for, which would actually be pretty much like my life in the countryside now but with more money and a bigger house (let's be honest, we all wish, hope and dream for that one day).

I now believed that I was being shipped off somewhere to make the best of a very bad situation and try and get my life back on track with all these new and sometimes quite intimidating people who talked about medical stuff a lot.

Different people kept coming in and out.

Drinks.

Pills.

Choices to make.

I kept asking questions to try and make sense of it and continued checking if people and pills were safe to take. I thought they had spiked my cup of tea with something.

What was going to happen next?

That time spent in this room scared the shit out of me. I went from tears to fears, from questions to exhaustion, in and out of rest and restlessness.

I felt so bad for my parents at this point, as if they need this kind of stress at their age.

What had I done!

Dad was getting things organised and kept asking about the ambulance, timings etc.

My chap had brought me a bag the previous night knowing I would be admitted, believing it would be somewhere nice for me to heal this breakdown. He'd done his best to pick out some jogging bottoms and random tops for me to wear, I imagine this was hard in itself as you know us girls we like to make sure we have organised outfits to wear as well as all of those lotions and potions we use.

Even the overnight bag was confusing me.

I didn't have my stuff that I wanted. It was all mismatched and jumbled. What was I going to do?

I decided to stay in the butterfly T-shirt and jeans which felt clammy and sweaty by this point. I felt really icky but all the thoughts of what may have happened took over any body odours! That said if you ever find yourself in a losing it kind of place have a bag packed just in case. You never know!

A useful list:

Your favourite uplifting book

Clean knickers

Facial wipes

Deodorant

Slippers

Your favourite comfy leggings

A nice comforting loose top

A hairbrush

Toothbrush and toothpaste

Shampoo and conditioner

An iPod or something to play music on

A pen and notepad

Seriously though, this was not a good place to be! They left a tiny little toothbrush and miniature toothpaste on the sink, I thought it was laced with sedatives to try and knock me out more.

I was really paranoid.

Paranoid about everything and still feeling very very frightened about what I was experiencing.

My emoji style faces were now of extreme sadness and I resigned myself to the fact that there was no game show, no good outcome, I'd totally blown it.

We waited.

Spoke a little.

Mum and dad doing their best to reassure me from their own place of disbelief. My face was scrunched up like a baby crying out for help and support.

Then it was time to go.

Chapter 5

From A Rock To A Harder Place

The ambulance was ready.

My beautiful healing retreat awaits!

I knew this wasn't the case at this point but still held onto some slight hope that all would come good.

I was wheeled out to the car park where an old well used ambulance was waiting for me to take me to 'The Ward'. I asked the two guys who were now in charge of me why we weren't going in one of the nice new ambulances, to which he told me this one would do the job.

I sat in the back with mum and dad.

I didn't know where I was at this point.

I started to see some familiar surroundings as they told me where I was being transferred to.

I looked around to see if I could spot some kind of tell-tale signs about the destruction that I had been imagining all weekend but everything looked normal (ish). It was me who wasn't the normal one.

It turns out that some small fortunes were in my favour. I was being transferred to a place which was actually on my mum and dad's direct bus route so it would be easy for them to visit me as they don't drive. I could have been sent anywhere in the country which would have made things even worse.

The old me would have been excited by the synchronicities and alignment but this new me couldn't muster up any form of pleased or happy about this let alone magic or excitement.

I kept asking them "what have I done wrong? Where are you taking me?"

Once again I started to feel a lot of fears about having to create a new life, I was also asking why they were doing this to me. I could sense my mum and dad were really upset but they did their best brave faces.

I just needed to try and figure all of this mess out. It had now been well over a week since I started to be involved in all of the stress with my friend. All those messages, all those people, all that out of control manic stuff and this was where I now found myself.

They reassured me that I would be ok and this place they were taking me would help me to put myself back together again, to heal myself.

It didn't feel right. Something within me was saying NO this isn't right. My gut instinct, my powerful women's intuition felt really off. Then we arrived. Unfortunately 'The Ward' included the word priest in it so that compounded my suspicions about a religious intervention for all my sins and that this life 'upgrade' certainly wasn't an upgrade in my mind.

My heart was racing!

My mind was racing!

Why was this happening?

Why wasn't anyone telling me anything?

Explaining stuff. To ease my aching brain.

I've had operations in the past where they guide you through what they are going to do every step of the way to make sure you feel relaxed and comfortable. I was now being treated like a time bomb ticking away waiting to explode at any given minute.

I think they wheeled me to the ward, I was very quiet at this point like I was being wheeled to my own personal judgment day.

What was going to happen next?

The ambulance men said I would be safe here but I knew this

THE DAY I GOT SECTIONED

area from when I was a child and it certainly wasn't a safe loving part of the world to be in let alone 'The Ward' that I was now going to be part of.

It turns out I was just up the road from where I spent the first six months of my life. It used to be a better area to live in but 40 years later it wasn't a very nice place at all.

I did think it was crazy that I found myself in this place again, maybe part of my rebirth?

Was I going to be put to sleep again but this time for real as in death? Reborn onto a paradise earth like what I was told when I was child?

Nope, sadly not. I would have been very sad if my existing life wasn't there waiting for me in paradise remembering that I thought my chap and my friends were long gone by this time.

'The Ward' was through various security doors to keep a check on who was coming and going, a little bit like you would expect a prison to be.

I vaguely recollect being sat in the corridor seeing a man crawling across the floor and shouting at the top of his voice, I assumed they were doing some kind of counselling or shamanic healing process allowing him to express his emotions in a safe and loving space. How very wrong I was. I've been involved in shamanic healing processes for a number of years, I even made my own drum from scratch. I know this kind of therapy can help you heal trauma but I wondered if some of the journeying I had done previously brought all of this on. I had also been calling life a shh-Manic process hinting at mental health issues previous to my breakdown. Is this what brought it on? I had done some drumming at my friend's the week before, maybe this didn't help?

I also thought I heard some music playing and wondered if they used music or art therapies to assist recovery. Wrong. Not that either.

I ached all over and felt really sick.

Maybe I was feeling so much more in my body because I was so sensitive?

I was covered in bruises too and my feet hurt from the dragging out of the house incident the previous day.

Life was on fast forward, so much had happened in such a short space of time and now I had even more of a crazy environment to try and settle into.

What if my Meniere's disease came on?

What if I was sick in here as well?

Thank goodness it didn't but I worried about this a lot and it took some of my own personal strengths to hold it all together.

When I've had Meniere's attacks (I prefer to call them episodes) in the past I'm like the living exorcist, projectile vomiting like someone has thrown me out of a plane with no parachute. It's not a nice disease (are any?) but that was the last thing I needed right now!

I had to keep it together the best I could. Put Meniere's into the mix with madness and I might end up here for life!

Chapter 6

Time To Settle In?

Mum and dad stayed with me, my chap had to go home to sort things out there. I wished he could have been there too as I relayed my story of the previous week's hell and what had unfolded which led to my serious lack of sleep and stress. I knew I had been seriously misunderstood, my chap could have helped me, what a shame!

He knew all the details but he wasn't there to back me up and mum and dad only knew what they'd seen since the previous day's unravelling.

The psychologist was only a young guy I would say probably mid to late twenties, I looked into his eyes to see how I felt about talking to him.

I believe eyes are our window to the soul, hence all my 'safe eye' checking. He seemed ok, he was on edge and looked tired but I'm sure I didn't help this with my out there story about what tipped me over the edge and led me to 'losing it'.

I wasn't sure about the two women behind him whom I think were nurses or psychologists too, I decided to go for it and share everything nonetheless.

I knew I was talking at him a million miles an hour but there was so much to offload my increasingly aching brain. I tried my best to trust the process and have the hope that once they heard how much I'd already been through that they would make sure I was ok, at least well cared for.

I remember him asking me if I often heard voices like this in my head. I explained that all of the shit had actually happened with my friend the week before and that I was terrified someone would get hurt, injured or even killed as it seemed so out of control.

I knew from the way he looked at me that it was all too much. Yes it was for me too I thought to myself.

I tried to explain that all I was sharing actually happened (bTW this was what happened before my own psychosis and all the stress of trying to make a seriously not ok situation ok again). I felt he didn't believe me. At this point I turned to ask my mum and dad if I was there because I was in trouble. Had I done something seriously wrong?

Was I hearing voices the week before?

Had I made it all up?

Had I imagined it all?

Was my friend dead?

Did I have to defend myself against that fire or the knife? Had I stabbed someone?

Surely not????

I wasn't sure. I got all kinds of strange flashbacks. Massive fear here.

This line of questioning really didn't help! Why did he ask if it was all voices in my head?

Did the cyber flashing conspiracy theorist guy hold me hostage and brainwash me to kill someone?

I'm not really sure where I went after that, it's difficult to remember. I felt like a small child who has been seriously misunderstood, or done something really naughty. Once again I was worrying about what they would do to me next.

I decided to find hope in the depths of darkness and trusted that the therapy room, the library he told me about (obviously I love to read and books are a huge part of my life), and that the music I thought I heard playing in the corridors were all part of this 'retreat' away from the previously experienced nightmares of life.

Maybe this was going to be good for me?

After all I had experienced, in my actual reality as well as all the stuff which came after that, maybe this was the best place for me.

Maybe it would be like a retreat, I could read lots of books, drink my herbal tea, do therapies, yoga, sing, dance, express myself through art and open honest counselling and one to one coaching.

I'm from a coaching background you see and have experienced lots of alternative therapies in my life as well as sharing said therapies with others. As I mentioned before I also enjoyed shamanic drumming and native American /South American stuff.

I felt a tiny glimmer of hope and decided to go with the flow of what was unfolding.

Surely they know what I need?

Hugs, love, support, being able to open up and talk to people who understood this stuff and all that nice and sometimes fluffy stuff.

Nope. Wrong again Liz.

It was shortly after the meeting with the psychologist that mum and dad left, my chap had already arrived and was told to wait in another room, no-one was telling him what was going off either.

At some point in between my parents being with me and seeing my chap I had to have some more checks, weight, blood pressure, tablets and some food.

It's a bit blurry here as my brain was obviously shouting NO MORE! SYSTEM OVERLOAD! SERIOUS SHUTDOWN IMMINENT!

I do remember my first experience of the canteen which was like something off a TV show set, the dinner ladies wheeling in the hot foods as everyone seemed to be frantically choosing what they wanted as quick as possible. I later learnt this was because anything hot or sharp was deemed dangerous and needed to be taken away ASAP. The toaster kept being locked away in a cupboard.

I didn't look around too much as I couldn't take any more but it was busy to say the least, people shuffling around everywhere no-one really looking at each other.

I felt a very strange vibe.

I couldn't deal with it.

It'll be ok. I'll feel better when I get to my room and get settled. Knowing myself well it always takes me a little time to settle into new surroundings as well as meeting and getting to know all of these new people.

I'm a very sociable person, I love to make new friends and I pride myself on being very open and honest, saying it how it is, down to earth Yorkshire lass with a touch of magic thrown in for good measure.

On a deeper level I think I knew at this point there certainly wasn't anything magical about this place but I had to keep things together and put a brave face on.

I mustered up my best emoji face for BRAVE!

I ate the most disgusting meat pasty I've ever experienced in my life, it was mostly made up of potato with some kind of ground beef, the chips were dry and hard, I struggled to swallow them.

The food tasted funny, I wondered if they'd put medication in it to keep us sedated?

Someone took me back to the visiting room.

I was so happy to see my chap was here! He hadn't died! I was filled with overwhelming relief! I held him tighter than ever before. I cried, he cried, we hugged.

I was still watching the people shuffling past the window on the door and wondering why people looked like zombies without the blood but for now I decided to worry about that later on.

I did my safety checks with my chap.

Are you safe?

Am I safe?

Are we all safe?

Is this place safe?

He did his best to reassure me as he didn't really have a clue either. It was all he could to keep me calm bless him!

I said I would be ok in here that it seemed ok, internal alarm bells ringing in my head! Regardless of what I felt I was stuck on this ward and there seemed to be nothing we could do. At least he was alive, I was alive and we didn't appear to be in any immediate danger.

Mum and dad had got the door to door bus service home. They were exhausted, I felt bad about causing all of this and hurting the people I love by bringing about such a terrible circumstance.

I continued to say sorry a lot, it was similar to how I felt the previous day. I said or did something I considered to be wrong, silly or daft and apologised. If I felt that someone didn't get me I said sorry over and over again. When I shouted things out I judged myself, I was highly sensitive and the remorse was massive.

SORRY

I'M SO SORRY!

SORRY! SORRY! I'M SOOOOOO SORRY!

I felt like a complete failure.

My self-judgment was on overdrive, I'd never felt so wrong in my whole life!

My chap had to go. Riding the wave of tears. I felt so sad. I felt so alone.

Chapter 7

Monday Evening Self-Orientation

I had my grey bag with my mishmash of stuff in it but decided that was way too much to think about for now so stayed in my existing clothes, butterfly top and jeans now more clammy than ever.

I wasn't really there.

That's how it felt.

I was trying to make sense of everything but nothing made much sense at all.

I was on my own now, my chap, my mum and dad, my friends had gone. I had created this situation and I had to deal with it.

I hate anything new dropping on me in my normal life, I've never been great with change and of course being out of my precious routine. I was fucked! Even then my now very quiet voice within said keep the faith Liz it'll all come good. You will be ok, find the earth angels, there must be some in here surely!

I'm usually a girl who looks for angel signs like little white feathers falling from the sky or a kind smile on a difficult day. I give them out lots too and have been known to run free hugs events locally as well as lots of other lovely supportive stuff. I do it to help people get through this thing called life with a bit more love, light and laughter. Life can be hard without support.

I kept checking peoples eyes. Were they kind?

Would they look after me?

I was on a mixed sex, 23-bed ward with a wide variety of patients from different ethnic backgrounds and religions. I came to understand during my stay they also had a wide variety of mental health issues most of which were much more serious than my breakdown. Everything I share here in this book is my own interpretation making the best sense I could of it all. As I said in the introduction, no offence meant, this was just my perspective at the time.

There is supposed to be an orientation onto the ward. At this point there was no way on earth my broken brain would retain anything let alone a new place to live!

Someone showed me around. I say this loosely as I don't really remember much, just that my room was 21 and that it had no name on the door. It was easy to remember as I used to run a course called 21 days of magic, ironic I know!

I also remember a very trippy looking room with a bath in the middle which had all kinds of taps and shower heads and buttons on it. This room was locked up, it definitely didn't feel safe and I wasn't about to ask to take one of my 'magical baths' any time soon. I thought I saw a picture of an old fashioned roll top bath on the wall behind it but it certainly wasn't very 'Pride and Prejudice'!

I don't think they showed me any toilets or showers, I wasn't sure about getting any more food or drinks and I didn't get a key fob pass for my room that day. The lock on my door was broken anyway so at least I could get in and out, when I dared to come out that was. I also felt really worried about other people being able to get in too!

I was left in the room.

I sobbed.

It was awful.

Now don't get me wrong here, I live in a TINY little cottage and I am a simple girl, never been a prima donna or anything which resembles that.

The room was clean but the energy was not.

It felt dark, dense and very very tense.

I sobbed some more in disbelief.

What am I doing here?

What on earth is going on?

Who's safe?

Am I safe?

Are they safe?

Is this place safe?

I was relieved the window opened so I could let some fresh air in, the windows were covered in perforated metal so if you got too close you couldn't really see out but at least light was coming in.

My view was eerie.

An old unused miniature football pitch with one of those dark grey fake concrete floors and a giant set of outdoor chess pieces strewn all over the place. The goals were all ripped apart, it looked like it hadn't been used for years and resembled something off a horror film.

Was this real?

Was I dead?

Where the hell was I?

What did I do to deserve this?

Was it some kind of prison for people who've gone mental?

I was only trying to help fix an unfixable situation which led me to no sleep and going out of my mind (literally) with worry and fear.

Alarms kept going off both on the ward and in my head.

I could hear lots of movement, people everywhere.

I felt afraid to leave my room.

I didn't know where to get a drink.

Where to shower.

Where my next food would come from.

Like I said maybe they did show me all of this but I don't remember. Surely when someone has just been admitted to this kind of horrendous place they could do with some extra support?

A kind face.

Someone to talk to.

Someone to say it's going to be ok, let me help you. You must be exhausted, let me give you a hug and a nice cuppa tea!

Nope.

My inner alarm bells in my ears were ringing at this point too, my tinnitus, which is part of the Meniere's disease, had started. Stress and tension bring it on so this was inevitable.

I also didn't have any of my Meniere's medication or my herbal tablets too. What would I do? I'd tried to tell them but no-one listened to me!

Chapter 8

The Information Overload Pack

In between my crying and sobbing I found an information pack on one of the shelves in my room. There was also an information board.

Like I didn't already have enough information overload, I thought I'd better take a look and try and fathom out what I needed to do to keep safe and well in this awful place.

In the information pack I was called a 'Service User' which I found very confusing. I hadn't chosen to be here, I hadn't picked this kind of service to use. I thought I was a patient, someone who was ill and was going to get better in here.

At some point during my stay I was given the analogy of someone breaking their leg and how it needs to be fixed and will then take time to heal.

Hummmmm. Give it some time Liz.

So I read the information pack, cover to cover a number of times. There were lots of leaflets too, when you opened the cover some were printed upside down which was also confusing.

Was this some sort of game?

Was I in one of those escape room games which people group book for stag or hen parties?

It felt like some kind of puzzle to solve.

I also had the game show thing playing out in my mind again, that old safety net!

Maybe something fabulous can still come from this living nightmare?

Maybe I was on the Michael MacIntyre Show and someone created this horrible pretend reality for the show and any minute now I would pop out of that box on the stage with everyone cheering and clapping because I had survived my ordeal and found my way out.

Or maybe Ant and Dec were waiting in the wings to congratulate me for getting through this and figuring out how to escape?

In between my studying up on my patient (or should that be service user) information I went to try and get a cuppa tea at some point. Bless my chap he'd brought my favourite tea tin with my herbal tea bags in as I don't drink too much caffeine to help with my balance.

I took some deep breaths and ventured out with my tea bag in hand.

A guy showed me the kitchen area and a hot water machine and some small polystyrene cups. At home I have a lovely big mug with rainbow love hearts all over it, I missed my mug.

No rainbows or love hearts here that's for sure.

I thanked him, he seemed ok.

I felt a little more comfortable.

I had my tea in hand.

Someone came up to me and asked me to do a pee sample. She seemed nice. Maybe it wasn't going to be as bad as I thought. I think it was around this time they gave me some more medication. I was asking if the tablets were safe, what were they giving me? Would it make me sick? What about the Meniere's?

I tried to explain that I had this condition and took medication for it but they didn't know how to spell it (Meniere's is named after the French guy who first suffered from extreme vertigo). I gave it up as a bad job and took the tablets.

Things started to get very strange from this point on. I will do my best to share what happened from my point of view with an understanding that everyone involved was doing their best (hopefully). As we all are.

Perfectly Imperfect in our human experience.

I spent a lot of time in my room alone listening to all the hustle and bustle of the ward and its service users outside. I was conscious my door wasn't locking and worried about who might come in. Faces kept appearing at the window of my door and shining a bright light into my room. I didn't have any way of telling the time but it felt like they were checking on me regularly.

It was getting dark. What should I do next? I was afraid of everything.

I read and re-read my 'Service User Information' leaflet.

It said I was in hospital under section 2 of the Mental Health Act 1983. That was 35 years ago! I thought to myself, things have changed a lot in the last 35 years why hasn't this?

I was five years old when this was created, we've evolved so much since then, why hasn't this system evolved too?

Maybe time for an update?

It said two doctors had examined me and think I have a mental disorder.

I JUST NEEDED TO EXPRESS WHAT HAD HAPPENED, GET IT OFF MY CHEST AND SLEEP!

It said I must stay there so the person in charge of my care could find out what was wrong with me. I thought I'd already explained this to the young psychologist guy that afternoon! Was no-one listening to me?

At this point I did actually wonder if I had some undiagnosed mental disorder as I know my emotions have always been a bit all over the place from since I was young but that's just part of life's ups and downs and round and arounds.

To this day no-one has officially told me what was 'wrong' with me. I chose to call it a nervous breakdown but after further research online since my release I find this term is no longer used. Psychosis is what I decided had happened due to lack of sleep and extreme stress. Since leaving the ward with five diazepam's (marzipan's as my dad called them) I have not required any more medication for my 'mental disorder' and take Kalms tablets or Rescue Remedy to deal with the anxiety, nightmares and flashbacks all of this has caused. Anyway more on that later.

Back to the paperwork. My brain was on fire at this point, I'm so glad I didn't spontaneously combust in there!

I checked the date of my release which appeared to be six weeks from that day, I was a little confused by what day or date I was on but knew it was Friday the 13th when all the previous sectioning stuff happened. I worked out it was the 16th but the date on my very official looking form was six weeks away!

What! I was going to be in here for six weeks!

The form said I could be kept there for four weeks.

HELP!!!! THEY HAD PUT THE WRONG DATE ON IT!

As I continued to read there was missing or unclear information. This form also said that my responsible clinician and other members of staff will talk to me about treatment and in most cases I had to accept their advice.

So far no-one was telling me anything very much at all. The scariest part of this form was the bit that said Electro-Convulsive Therapy could be given! OH MY GOODNESS! THAT'S WHAT THAT STRANGE BATH WAS FOR! ELECTRO-CUTING PEOPLE!

There was information about appealing saying I had to ask the hospital managers to do this. Who were they? Who was my responsible clinician? Who was my nurse? No-one had told me anything.

It told me I must not leave or staff would stop me or bring me back. I couldn't even remember where the toilets were let alone the exit!

There was a 'what happens next' section it said my responsible clinician would tell me when I was well enough to leave. It said they may decide I need to be in hospital for longer which would be section 3 of the 35 year old Mental Health Act at which point

I would be given another leaflet (I wondered if that one would be printed the right way up!) I could then be kept for up to six months. I felt that black hole in the floor swallowing me up again!

I HAD TO GET OUT OF HERE!

The appeal information said I would have to write to the hospital managers but I didn't even have any paper or a pen.

Was I jumping the gun?

Yes, probably but this is how I do things. Efficiently and quickly, especially when things don't feel right and this definitely didn't. It also said my nearest relative could contact the hospital managers but the nearest relative box was left blank.

Once again it felt like a game show. Surreal. Unreal. Something concocted by some twisted yet ever so slightly funny production team for entertainments sake! Oh well at least if I win this game I might get a prize for my efforts. Maybe I would win some money!

These feelings were harking back to when I was giving a lot of my time and offering support for free, as well as doing lots of other voluntary stuff. I loved doing this at the time but hadn't realised I was draining myself and not receiving much financial compensation.

I read about the tribunal which said I could only appeal within the first 14 days of the 28 days I was kept in hospital. They would hold a hearing and apparently someone would come and talk to me, this sounded like a good idea as no-one was telling me what on earth was happening.

I was starting to feel more and more trippy, I wondered if it was the game show again. Did I need to go and call my chap and tell him I wanted to appeal and that we only had another 13 days left? (13 lucky for some!). I wondered if all the other patients aka service users were appealing too and if I should do it nice and quickly so as to win the imaginary prize.

It also spoke of an independent mental health advocate who would be able to help me get more information about my care and treatment. There were numbers to phone but I didn't even have a phone plus it was too late for that. I didn't know the time but it must have been past 9pm as it was getting dark outside.

It said that a copy of this leaflet would be given to my nearest relative but as I mentioned previously the box for whom my nearest and dearest is had been left blank. I thought about my brother and all the 1000s of miles away he was, that wouldn't work.

Who was my nearest blood relative?

Who could help me?

It said I could change this person if I needed to, I had to find a phone and call my chap.

It also said I could send and receive letters, but as I said before I didn't have a pen or paper.

Apparently there is a code of practice too. The staff have to consider what the code says and I could ask for a copy of the code.

What was this code? How would it affect me?

It all sounded really complicated plus by this time I was freaking out again. My breath was short and my heart was racing ten to the dozen. How on earth could I possibly cope with all of this information overload upon information overload!!

There was a note on the last page about complaining about my care and treatment. I decided as soon as I could get hold of a pen I would start a list on the inside cover of this information pack, to keep track of all the things I wanted to complain about.

There was also lots of leaflets to go through about smoking policies. Smoking was banned but that's another story as I would see when I started to visit the 'Zen garden' also known as the smoking area.

Every now and again I would pop my head outside my door, avoiding eye contact with any dangerous looking people and check on my surroundings to try and piece things together.

I read the mutual expectations list a few times, my head was pounding and I was finding it difficult to focus.

I've added some of my responses which come from the total of my 10 day stay on 'The Ward'. This is just a taster, lots more to come on the following pages but at least it gives you a feel for what I was dealing with.

I also want to say at this point, once again I know everyone was doing their best and have been told that any staff who work in this kind of high stress environment become desensitised to what's happening around them. No finger pointing intended this was just my point of view from where I stood.

Our Mutual Expectations:

1. On admission, all patients will be orientated to the ward and receive an information pack.

Yes, thank you for leaving that in my room, it would have really helped if someone could have sat down and gone through it all with me. Also please can the orientation be after the 'service users' have had some shut eye. Maybe, just maybe some of us have gone through enough at this point.

K.I.S.S

- Keep

- It

- Simple

- Stupid!

2. We will listen to each other and speak to each other with respect and courtesy.

Yes, I was trying my best but no-one seemed to be listening to me. Also the other patients, 'service users' or inmates (not sure what to call them at this point) didn't always seem to want to use nice respectful language.

3. We will try and be sensitive to the fact that others are unwell.

Yes, that's fine, I understood but no-one seemed to be showing much sensitivity to me.

4. We will not be aggressive to one another and will always try to talk in a calm manner.

Aggression isn't in my nature, I recalled the water throwing incidents and wondered if that counted, as well as the times I accidentally swore but apologised straight after on most occasions, I may as well say sorry for the swearing in this book now too. It's the best way I can express my feelings as I share them here with you.

I had so much mixed up energy pent up inside me I needed to cry out for help! It was very hard to remain calm when my head and heart were racing at a million miles an hour.

Stay focused Liz.

(The next bit had some mixed up wording, will and nurse were the wrong way around)

5. Your allocated will nurse introduce themselves to you at the start of the shift and staff will always wear i.d. badges when on the ward.

What was a will nurse? I know it was a simple grammatical error and I've probably made lots in this book but this freaked me out, did I need to write a will in case I died in here?

Let's not get started on the name badge situation! Some wore them around their neck, some were upside down, some were covered in stickers and all of the photos were so out of date no-one looked like who they said they were. There was also a notice board in the entrance to the ward with a display of pictures, job titles and names of the people who worked there. The pictures must have been years out of date as no-one looked the same, some of the pictures were missing too. I looked at this often but it wasn't clear at all.

6. You will be given some one to one time with your allocated nurse during the day. They will be expected to have a knowledge of your care plan. Please try and use this time in a positive way.

This never happened. Given the chance I would have used it in a positive way. I was wide open for some fucking positivity after all the negativity experienced until this point. I never saw a care plan either.

7. Wherever possible, at least one member of staff will be

available on the open ward.

There always seemed to be loads of people about but I wasn't sure who anyone was. There were a lot of people sat in an office swinging on chairs and lots of people running about with alarms and worried looking faces.

8. Staff will keep the office door open, unless discussing confidential matters or when no staffs available.

Staffs? Grammar again, but still I wondered if they would hit me with a big staff if I didn't follow their expectations. I thought I was allowed to go into the office, but sometimes I was told to get out.

9. Staff will respond to your requests in a timely manner and give explanation where there is delay. You can expect an explanation if your request is denied.

Oh no! I really hoped none of my requests were denied. They sometimes were but I got used to that.

10. Whilst on the ward you will be informed about the activities and therapies available to you and these can help with your recovery.

The whiteboard in the main area had the previous week's dates on which included Friday the 13th that dreaded day when life became too much. I could hardly read the red writing on this board but it didn't look as if much had happened the week

THE DAY I GOT SECTIONED

before. I wondered if the dates were right and I had died and this was some kind of mental hell? I told the staff on a number of occasions that the dates were wrong but no-one updated them. I was never informed about any activities or therapies during my stay.

11. Your care team will include you in all aspects of your care and treatment. With your consent we will involve your family and others who support you.

During my stay I never met a 'care team', yes nurses and lots of agency staff along the way but I wouldn't say this was a team.

T.E.A.M

Together

Everyone

Achieves

More

Hummmmm. Some of the staff were lovely and I appreciated them very much. No-one asked me to give consent for family or my chaps involvement, if they had I would have consented a million percent but no-one was involved. My chap had to chase and chase for anything sorting.

12. In order for the ward to run smoothly, there has to be routine. We will try and respect this, e.g. mealtime,

medicine rounds, visiting times etc.

There were no rounds. Medicine was a knock on the door and an authoritative voice shouting medicine or meal time. If you were out and about wandering the corridors it was usually a swift shout to attention. Sometimes I would notice a queue forming and join it just in case.

Points 13 & 14 were repeated and highlighted in bold like a mantra so I thought these must be very important points to take in.

13. We should all be mindful to keep lights and noise to a minimum at night.

14. We should all take responsibility to ensure the ward is kept clean and tidy.

13. We should all be mindful to keep lights and noise to a minimum at night.

14. We should all take responsibility to ensure the ward is kept clean and tidy.

Mindful. Yes my mind was very full thank you very much and now I thought I had to start cleaning the place up too which would have been a very long job to say the least! I felt like it was my responsibility.

It ended with the following statement:

We will all work towards a positive and hopeful

environment, working together to support your recovery.

I would change this, as follows:

We will add to your high levels of stress, panic, anxiety and confusion and give you various tests, trials and tribulations to try and tip you over the edge in case you haven't fallen off the edge of the ledge already.

I know I sound harsh but lots of these words are shared from the place of panic and fear I found myself in on the first night, the others come from over a week of my life which was spent in this place observing what was happening.

There was also an infection prevention and control leaflet which sounded very official. It made me wonder if this was because some major disaster had happened in the outside world. Sounded scary but I nodded as I read it to say I would do my bit as much as possible.

There was a leaflet about rights for voluntary patients which was the one printed upside down. It made me feel dizzy but I wasn't there through choice but still decided I'd better read it anyway.

Then came the 'Welcome to The Ward Information for Service Users'. This was a 10 page, doubled-sided printed document which had the most horrendous picture of a creepy looking man on the front, with an innocent young looking woman smiling at him.

It looked like an anti-rape picture.

FREAK ME! THIS IS TOO MUCH TO TAKE!

I flicked through it as I was starting to feel even more weirded out, the first page I came to was entitled 'House Rules'. I had to make sure I knew 'the rules' and keep myself safe in this horrible place! So I flicked over it and went to try and get another cup of tea with my ever increasing shaking hands, finding it hard to even hold my tea by this point let alone do anything else.

At some point during the evening (maybe at this time) I was asked to see the phlebotomists, they were in the same place medication was dished out which was a bit like an old broom cupboard where everyone was ushered in about four times a day.

As soon as I saw the phlebotomists I knew something was off! I knew I must be imagining things now! What I saw were two men dressed in sexy white PVC nurses outfits waving a needle in the air! Red lipstick 'n all! WTF!

Emoji faces kicked back in at this point.

NO! NO! NO! I'm not going in there.

Who are they?

What are they doing?

Someone was also trying to give me a form I needed to fill out, it was something to do with benefits, my brain was starting to melt and run out of my ears by this point. More paperwork? REALLY?

MAJOR SYSTEM OVERLOAD, PLEASE STEP AWAY IMMEDIATELY! SHE'S GONNA BLOW!!

I ran back to my room! I looked at the information board on the wall which involved lots more confusing information and sentences that didn't make much sense.

There were instructions on how to use the safe. At the best of times I'm a bit of a technophobe but this was not the point to start setting safe codes and pressing buttons.

Was this the code which the staff had?

Could they help me?

Should I go and ask for a code? Will that be the code that gets me out of this place?

I decided the safe was not safe.

Nor was I!

Nor was this place!

In between all of my reading and investigating, different people kept coming to my door window peering in at me and shining a bright light in my face. I was being watched, they were observing me. Why? What had I done?

Every time I felt someone's presence I would stop what I was doing and try to look natural otherwise they may electrocute me in that awful bath or keep me in here forever!

Act as normal as you can Liz.

That wasn't possible. I wasn't sure what normal was anymore. Plus I needed a wee and daren't go to the toilet, at this point I wasn't even sure if I had been to the toilet since I'd left casualty! I had but the hours were merging, I was more confused and scared than I had ever been in my whole life. My day to day needs for comfort such as a simple pee and drink of water were too hard to work out! HELP!

Chapter 9

The Bad Trip

In my normal life in my countryside cottage, well let's say semi-normal, I love to walk in nature and often ask the angels what my next best steps are, I was too far gone for this so decided I should simply follow my feelings.

I felt even stranger than I had felt before.

Something was off.

I reverted back to flitting between massive fear for mine and others safety and the game show or escape room competition.

I must go phone my chap and say I want to appeal, I want the tribunal! I want out! This is a game! This is scary! This is wrong on so many levels!

I OFFICIALLY ANNOUNCE I AM OUT!

Now where's my prize?

I went to the office to phone home.

I didn't even know what time it was at this point. I gingerly and as politely as possible popped my head through the office door and said I needed to phone my chap, Cat. Cat is his nickname, this caused some confusion during my stay so I had to revert back to calling him Ian once I realised I sounded like I wanted to phone my cats or that my cats were coming to visit me in the ward. Oh dear!

They said I could use the phone.

I had written the number at the top of the patient information sheet in case I forgot it as I could feel my thoughts getting more and more confused minute by minute. I also wrote my own number down in case I had to try that as he had my mobile phone with him at home.

The staff were very to the point, no softness or smiles. At the end of the day they were simply getting a job done and it was late.

I was told to dial 9 for a line out.

Oh no! Would 9 call the police again?

Was it some sort of code to alert the police about me or was it a secret 9 (999) call to let the bombers and terrorists outside know that I had sussed them out and I was in charge of all of these people's lives.

I felt that big fear again.

The stuff I was processing at the weekend was back. It was awful. I felt like I was sinking into the ground again. This time I couldn't understand why it was happening and I couldn't control what happened next.

On a side note, as I write this here today, I am still waiting for my medical reports and documentation as on the last day I was told that the medication they gave me clashed with the existing medication I was taking for Meniere's disease. I had been taking my existing medication prior to my breakdown so it was still in my system.

SHOCKER!

I am sure this is the case as I would describe the way I felt as extremely trippy like someone had given me LSD and programmed me in for the worst trip of a lifetime.

I did once experiment with LSD when I was 15 and it felt similar to this but this was worse and went on for most of the night!

I was now beyond scared!

I put the phone down, I couldn't call him!

I ran back to my room and put all the information stuff away. I hid the pack underneath my bag to make sure no-one took it off me.

I had to focus on the people watching me and make sure I was safe.

They were at my door again, lights flashing, alarms, overwhelment.

I went to the window.

Was this real?

The broken football goals, the giant chess pieces.

The last week or so and everything that happened.

The crimes.

The bombs.

The fear!

Was it all true!

They were at my window again!

Bright light shining in! Who were all these people?

I had to do something!

Was it the pills they gave me?

The blue pill stuff kicked back in but this time it was even more scary and my whole body was shaking and sweating.

The sink in my sparse and unfriendly room was very strange, it looked like a face with the tap in the middle as the nose. To the left a big red button for hot water and to the right a big blue button for cold water looked like eyes.

Press the red button Liz!

Keep pressing the red button and you will be saved!

I remembered my feelings about the food I'd eaten earlier in the evening being spiked with some kind of strange drug, maybe the red button for hot water would cancel it out and stop these out of control feelings.

I started to move around and dance.

I needed to move and shake these feelings off.

I needed to get grounded.

I also needed to pee so thought the dancing would help this too!

I was dizzy. I was so frightened and there was no-one to help me.

All I could do was dance and start to shout and sing.

It's hard to remember all the finer details at this point which doesn't surprise me looking back, I bet it doesn't surprise you either!

Keep dancing and singing Liz, you will be ok.

I grabbed my herbal tea tin and emptied out the contents on the windowsill still conscious I wasn't allowed to make any mess and trying to follow the new rules I was learning. I took out one of the

THE DAY I GOT SECTIONED

tea bags and popped it in my new tea tin 'cup'.

I kept filling the tin with hot water from the red button drinking the luke warm tea concoction thinking it would counteract any blue pill related stuff. The tin was leaking water all over the floor and all over me as I continued to drink the tea water and dance as hard as I possibly could.

I was so hot at this point I threw some water over myself for good measure. The floor was slippy!

People were at my door.

I danced to the door and started to hide underneath the window, jigging about and popping up to look out every few seconds.

People everywhere creeping up to my door, rushing about, sirens and alarms going off.

I started to copy the sound of the sirens.

"WOOOOO WOOOOOO WOOOOOO!"

As loud as I possibly could to alert people to get back. They were still coming for me.

"WOOOOOO WOOOOOOO WOOOOOO!"

They were coming to get me!

I'd fucked up BIG TIME now. This was it!

I remembered Peaky Blinders and how it seemed to help me the day before so started to do impressions of the powerful gypsy woman who is one of the characters.

I opened the door and looked around.

People everywhere. Looming towards me!

Fuck me! I was so scared!

As they came nearer I shouted in a very deep very loud voice "SHUT THE FRONT DOOR" and slammed the door shut.

"GET BACK"

"WOOOOOO WOOOOOO WOOOOOO"

Then I started singing again.

Tribal songs, Asian music, opera, whaling, chanting, anything I could think of.

I must sing for all nations for all people!

I have to stop these atrocities happening!

No idea where all of this came from. It was like someone else had taken over my voice box and control of my body.

This went on for what felt like hours.

"SHUT THE FRONT DOOR!"

"YOU'RE NOT SAFE! I'M NOT SAFE! NO-ONE IS SAFE! WOOOOOO WOOOOOO WOOOOOO!"

"ARE YOU SAFE? AM I SAFE? IS THIS PLACE SAFE?"

It was exhausting! Make no wonder I lost loads of weight with all that exercise.

If they had popped me on a podium in a nightclub I would have danced all night and most probably danced these demons out of me too.

From what I could make out they needed to catch me and make me stop as people kept trying to grab me or calm me down.

Eventually I opened the door and looked around the corridor. It was dark but beyond all of the people trying to catch me I could see a figure in the corridor. It was my chap wearing a horse's head mask (this was one of the emojis he had sent me and we joked about before all of this happened).

I wasn't laughing or joking at this point.

I saw the figure of a woman carrying a knife looking like that creepy dead girl in the film The Ring.

I was imagining things but they felt so real at the time!

I was beyond frightened!

I kept looking around at everyone in the corridor. Men and

women of all ages and backgrounds. Some looked scared some looked angry.

Who was safe?

I started to try and get eye contact with some of the younger looking women who I think were trainees. 'The Ward' was also a training place for people too, I guess that's why it was also so busy.

I saw a girl who looked a little like my spiritual friend (oh yes she was back in a new form).

I asked if she was an earth angel and if she would help me. I started shouting my friend's name at the top of my voice and as she rushed away from me I pretended we were at the fire walk again and I was cheering her on.

A fleeting thought. Did my spiritual friend die at the fire walk? Did she go up in flames?

I was back in the modern day witch hunt scenario!

Was I going to be stabbed?

Best to keep dancing and shouting.

So that's what I did. I never laid a hand on anyone as far as I can remember, some of my language may have sounded aggressive but I was more terrified than I had ever been in my life.

I looked like I'd peed myself at this point as I had water all down my front and was sweating like a pig on a hog roast. My legs were shaking but I couldn't stop, it was like someone else had taken over my body.

I must keep moving, dancing, singing and shouting.

I went out into the corridor which felt like something from a horror film at this point.

I was still shouting for my friend to come back from the fire walk.

Other people were around me. I kept trying to look into their eyes. Some had dilated pupils probably due to the stress of what I was doing!

"SHE SMOKES DOPE!" I shouted!

This was connected with smoking Marijuana myself. It was for medicinal purposes, which was to help with the Meniere's disease, dare I say, as well as a little bit of social herb too. Maybe this was why I felt so bad? I hadn't had any for a while but won't ever touch it again that's for sure!

Another nurse was lovely but she had a Fitbit on, I recognised her from earlier, she was the one who asked me to do a pee sample. I did know where the toilets were! I could see them from my room! I was too scared to go to the loo by now and knew they would grab me if they got too near.

I guessed from her Fitbit that she might do Slimming World, before my breakdown I was attending meetings and had managed to release over a stone in weight. I'd dabbled with being vegetarian and vegan for a while too which was hard on Slimming World as everyone seemed to be eating that Quark stuff which I think tastes awful and doesn't really feel like a nourishing or healthy food. Also a lot of the diet is meat based so it became hard to do, I felt triggered by this and struggled with it.

"SHE DOES SLIMMING WORLD!" I Shouted!

"SLIMMING WORLD IS POISONOUS!"

I needed to warn her! I also started asking for a Snickers to prove that it was ok to eat chocolate and we don't have to beat ourselves up or obsess over 'Syns' (or should that be sins?) and points and such like. No offence to weight loss groups they've helped me so much throughout my life but at this point I had fallen out with any kind of controlling energy.

On a side note I did manage to get my Snickers bar later that night when I was shouting about having low blood sugar levels. I also had my dad bring me a multipack of them to hide in my room in case I ran out of food. I wish I hadn't as the very strange marketing campaign at the time meant the wrappers had negative words printed on them. They said things like 'Loser', 'Wasted', 'Knackered' and 'Confused', bad timing for me and maybe for others too! I wondered if they were special mental hospital bars to trigger us.

Why on earth would you want such words printed on your food? What a ridiculous marketing campaign! A note to all marketeers out there: Please consider how this kind of marketing affects people who may be going through a rough time!

I preferred to fill my food with positive energy before I ate it! In the end I left said chocolate bars in the kitchen for someone else to eat, I was worried about what they said on the wrappers tipping someone over the edge but I had to get rid of them!

Back to the madness of that Monday night:

I needed to get back into my room, I was feeling more and more out of control. I ran back into what I thought was my room but accidentally burst into the poor lady's room next door to me, apparently she had been in mental health hospitals for over thirty years, I'm sure it wasn't the first time it had happened, nevertheless they should have got those bloody locks sorted!

I came back out.

"SORRY! SORRY! SORRY! I CAN'T STOP!

ARE WE SAFE?

ARE YOU AN ANGEL?

WILL YOU HELP ME?

I'M SORRY ABOUT THE SLIMMING WORLD STUFF I JUST NEED TO EAT SOME CHOCOLATE!"

I can't remember how I got to the blue padded plastic mattress room (sounds inviting doesn't it?!). The official name is the seclusion room. At a later meeting, after my release, I was told this was usually only for very violent or aggressive people who can't be contained.

That said there was no controlling me now, the singing went up a notch and the dancing had become more like a raver on an all night bender!

I continued to ask if we were safe. A smiley lady with neat hair and well done make-up came up to me, she said something about touchstone, unbeknown to me this was the name of the advocacy service, I thought she was from the TV crew! I connected touchstone with the film company. She was trying to give me another form to fill out or something else to read. More paperwork again? Really? Come on now, enough is enough!

I decided she wasn't safe.

"YOU'RE A JEHOVAH'S WITNESS GET AWAY!"

Oh dear, that one popped back in to say hello again. Bless the poor woman. I have to make an official apology here today to everyone involved in my reinterpretation of some strange horror film / game show production. It was not me it was the pills.

Either that or my completely overloaded brain which was about to explode.

I daren't do the head exploding emoji to tell them what was happening. Once again I thought every time I did it someone would be blown up for real in the outside world.

My main aim was escape! If I can get out I can save everyone!

Somehow I ended up in that awful room with four plastic blue chairs and a blue plastic padded mattress on the floor. HELP!

Chapter 10

The Seclusion Room

There was a set of swinging doors ahead of me and a big black door behind me.

Was that my escape route?

We had to get out in time before the bomb went off. I had to do something, I felt like this was all my fault!

One of the male nurses was starting to fall asleep so I sang my interpretation of tribal songs to him. I was trying to be politically correct and sing people songs from their ethnical background. I am sure I was seriously misunderstood at this point and thought to be racist which, once again, I will confirm I am not and have never been.

I was singing bangra style music to one of the other guys, I thought they had knives by the side of their chairs as they were slouched back with their hands by the side of the chairs. There was lots of eye-rolling and smirking happening too as this went on for hours, or at least I think it did as I had no time telling device at this point.

More people kept coming and going, I was telling them who was safe to stay and who was not but as they left I felt immense and intense remorse as I thought I'd sent them to their death.

"NO COME BACK! SORRY SORRY SORRY!"

I kept on dancing and singing.

I was told I was going to have to stop at some point or I would make myself ill. I think I was already way beyond ill.

I tried to force my way through the big black door in one last attempt to win the escape room contest, or pop out onto a stage with the TV audience clapping and laughing. The door was locked.

My heart sank. What would I do next?

This was it now. No way out!

Not sure exactly what happened next but from the information sheet I was given on the morning of my release sometimes the sedatives they use can be administered as a pessary. I felt like someone had put something in my bum, maybe they had, maybe they hadn't. My imagination was going through all kinds of scenarios, probably picked up from films or TV I had watched.

In my mind I had to protect myself, for some reason I had a pair of spare knickers in my jeans pocket, not sure when or how they got there, I must have picked them up in my madness.

I'm just going to say it like it is.....

I started to try and pull something out of my bum, a pessary? Not sure but I felt I needed to check what was up there..... I think I put whatever I pulled out into my mouth. URGH! I felt ashamed.

They were shouting at me, "NO NO NO!"

"Elizabeth calm down".

I'm Liz. Elizabeth is my Sunday name.

Whilst dancing around I started to try and push the spare knickers up my bum. Ouch!

I think they thought I had shit myself but it was my spare knickers. I thought I had a little bit of shit in my mouth, I kept saying sorry my breath smelt so bad and showing them my teeth.

At this point I think I peed myself and felt a sense of relief followed by deep embarrassment!

Everyone had blue gloves on.

This room was very blue, very clinical.

Another earth angel, a kind nurse with nice eyes kept telling me I was safe, she looked exhausted, so was I.

I kept making everyone tell me they were safe.

Safety checks went on for a while.

Are you safe?

Am I safe?

Are you safe?

Am I safe?

Yes.

Yes.

I was crying lots too. So much sadness about this awful situation I was in.

Somehow they managed to grab me by my arms and legs and pin me down to the blue padded mattress in the corner of the room.

I think there were six people at this point and it hurt. They had a very tight hold of me and severely added to the previous day's police induced bruises.

Someone started to pull my jeans and my pants down.

Was I going to be raped?

They injected me.

I screamed!

After this they tried to get me over to the toilet to clean me up, I fished the spare knickers out of my bum crack, I felt so ashamed and wrong.

There was a nice older lady who knelt down to take my jeans off and tried to soothe me.

She said her knees were hurting. I felt so bad! I had created this mess. It was all my fault.

I'm not sure how I got back to my room but I remember the nice lady whose knees hurt sitting in the chair at the side of my bed until everything went black and I slept.

Thank goodness for sleep.

Chapter 11

The Walk Of Shame

I woke up the next day filled with very deep very dark feelings and emotions. The once happy go lucky Liz was gone. I wept my heart out.

What would happen next?

I needed to know. I had to somehow pick myself up, dust myself off and find my inner strength. I needed the toilet. I needed a shower.

I needed to wash everything away.

I went to the toilet, fortunately I could see it from my door window as I felt disorientated and had forgotten where everything was.

Fast as you can Liz.

Was someone watching me whilst I was on the toilet having my morning poo? How embarrassing! I took some comfort in thinking it wasn't as bad as last night though!

Why were they watching me?

Who were all these people?

Once again there were people everywhere.

I figured out that the staff moved fast and are often quite erratic and the service users shuffled so I decided I had best slow down and join in the zombie ward shuffle. Maybe it was the medication mix up but I still felt quite hyper at this point.

Back in my room I looked into the mirror which was a piece of reflective plastic on the wall, I guess to stop people smashing the glass to use for suicide attempts. It made my face look distorted like I was in a hall of mirrors. My hair was greasy and frizzy, it looked like it was thinning, was the medication making it fall out? I checked and it seemed to be ok.

I brushed my teeth, cried some more and decided to get a nice herbal tea bag out and go to get some hot water. The tea I drink has lovely little messages on the tags, which I had now started to pull off the string and save on my windowsill by way of trying to lift my low spirits.

This morning's tea said 'sing from your heart' talk about ironic!

I thought I would give it to one of the staff who I was singing at in the horrible blue room by way of apology.

I found a tea tag on the floor from the night before, it was soggy and ripped but you could still read what it said. "Tranquility and dignity last forever". I had flashbacks to the night before and the scene I made.

Why did that happen?

It took me back to the Sunday at my parent's house when my mum was showing me her little Penguin Pride and Prejudice journal she wrote magical little things in. On the back of the book was a poem which said we should be dignified yet flippant. Mum had kept saying this to me, be dignified but flippant.

I would try my best to be more dignified in this undignified place, and would definitely be more dignified than I was the night before. I've always been quite sarcastic and humorous and as you can see I am a big believer that laughter is the best medicine. That wasn't the case on the ward though!

I wondered if what happened the night before was real. Did I really do all of that?

On my way for hot water I saw one of the guys from the seclusion room incident in the office, I walked in to give him the sing from your heart tea tag and apologise at which point I was told to get out.

"Oh I just came to give you this! Sorry!"

I explained myself and apologised again but he didn't seem to care or give me any sort of confirmation I had done the right thing. I still felt very paranoid.

Toughen up Liz. Stop being nice. Stop being weak and crying you need to sort yourself out I thought.

At some point I think I had some toast but was still unsure if it was laced with some kind of strange drugs after what happened the previous day. I was hungry I would eat what they gave me for now.

I got a phone call that morning too. It was my dad. I was directed to a phone box in a tiny little room with swinging doors and big windows, people shuffled past as I told my dad how scared I was and asked when they were coming as well as asking him to bring food.

I was reeling stuff off, my voice was nearly gone due to the night before but I knew my dad could hear the panic as I spoke. I was being watched so I did my best to keep calm and carry on. People kept sliding past the windows and staring at me.

The little Liz inside was way out of her depth now but something told me I had to get a grip, grow up, find my way around, start to be stronger and take note of what was really going off.

After the call I decided to venture into the 'Therapy Room', I wasn't greeted with the warm welcome I expected and no-one had invited me in but as the door was open I assumed it would be ok.

There was a woman in there waving a huge pair of scissors about which scared me, she looked to be cutting up materials for some kind of craft project. Was she a member of staff or was she one of the inmates?

There was a guy in there too with long hair, a beard and lots of skull tattoos on his arm, he reminded me of the Dr Death stuff. I tried to breathe as deeply as I could and focus upon what kind of therapy might help me, obviously the scissors weren't.

BTW I love tattoos, I have a full back piece of a geisha girl which took 30 hours, I also like long hair and beards and in normal circumstances don't have anything against scissors but once again it was all too much.

I am into alternative therapies and have taken part in lots of retreats and such like over the years, some way out stuff too. This was very different to any kind of therapy room I had experienced previously.

I remembered how my mum's therapy colouring booked helped a few days ago and sheepishly asked if they had any. The guy pointed to some books on the side. He was sorting some felt tip pens and putting them in order with the pen lid at one end, tips at the other. He said he had OCD so needed to make sure they were neat, I wondered if he was one of the service users too and I'd got things mixed up.

There was a lovely pack of glitter ink pens, I asked if I could use them and he said they weren't open so I asked if I could use the others. He seemed ok with this, I asked if I could take some to my room as I didn't feel safe at this point. I even asked the lady if the scissors were a good idea she seemed to panic and locked them away in a cupboard.

Maybe she thought I was going to use them?

I grabbed a full box of pens and a unicorn colouring book which also had nice quotes in it and legged it back to my room as fast as possible.

My door still wasn't locking, maybe my antics the night before didn't help but it was already broken anyway. I also queried why my name wasn't on my door and why I didn't have a key pass.

I'd managed to retrieve my slippers from the previous evening by asking one of the cleaners if she could find them as I had no idea where they would be. At this point the cleaners seemed like the friendliest safest people so I went with that. On another occasion, I asked the cleaner if she wanted an Angel Card reading but she said no which made me feel upset, it was as if she had been told not to interact with me too much, maybe she thought I wasn't safe?

I decided to move my room around and pushed the chair beside the window so at least I could sit and face away from the door where the faces kept peering in. I also didn't want to be staring at the blank walls or worse still the notice board and all the confusing information.

I knew I needed to do more research but decided to colour for a while and ponder my dismal view out of the window.

A few of the unicorns were already coloured in, the lines had been missed and most were just scribbled over in one colour. I wonder who had used this book before me, it made me feel sad.

So I coloured in unicorns and cried.

This lasted for a little while then I decided to use the biro pen I had also borrowed and start to take some notes. I needed to remember what day and date of the month I was on and log what was happening each day as none of it felt right. Something had to be done and I may as well try and sort the issues I had whilst I was in here, both to help my stay and maybe others who got sent there in the future.

I love to have a job to do. I love a purpose, without one I feel lost.

I started with day one and made notes on the official section 2 form, underlining the points which were unclear and the parts I felt I wanted to take action on.

I made the notes on the inside cover of the information pack, part of me wondered if I should start counting the days with lines and crosses on the wall but this felt a little bit too much like what someone would do in prison.

There were so many notes to take that the clear spaces were filling up fast. I decided to go and top my tea up, there was a guy in a shirt and tie near my room, he looked like an office bod, maybe he was part of the management team.

Ten years earlier I was a senior manager myself so I knew what it could be like up there in the ivory tower, it must have been worse when in relation to a mental ward like this.

I did my best to remain calm without too much panic in my voice as I told him my door wasn't locking and I didn't have my key pass. He was flustered and red in the face, was he scared of me or the other patients? Was I being erratic or not asking in a calm manner, I think I was. I'm assuming now it was the environment which made him uneasy, it made me feel that way too.

I wondered where my other clothes were from last night. I'd sort that later, I'd asked my dad to bring some stuff and when I felt a little more confident I called my chap using the office phone to put in some orders for food and clothes. Each day he started to bring more and more things in for me to make it feel at least a little bit more like home.

He thought I would only be in there a few days as he knew all I needed was sleep but that wasn't the case, once you are on the ward you are in the system as we found out first hand.

During one of my outings for a tea top-up the main area with the green plastic sofas seemed to get extra crowded, what was going on?

Where were all these people coming from?

The day before I was asking to check people's name badges and pictures to make sure they were staff, as I said the pictures were all outdated so not many of them looked like their badge. Some had stickers all over them so you couldn't really check, some were worn around the front of their chest which made it easier, others were clipped to the side of trousers so it was more awkward to check.

Who were all these people?

A kind looking guy dressed in a smart relaxed chino fashion approached me. He told me his name and that he was an advocate and could help me, he said it was the day to see the doctor.

This was new to me.

I asked if he was safe.

I was starting another slight panic attack so took in some extra breaths. He said he was safe and could help me but I remembered seeing a picture of the two advocates on a poster on the main notice board and he didn't look like either of them.

I wasn't sure what to do, I was looking around frantically trying to find someone who could confirm who he was, everyone was too busy, people going this way and that. Patients all around me.

I think I walked off at this point, someone told me my parents were here and I would be having a meeting.

A meeting sounded promising, maybe I could get some of my many queries answered. I went back to my room to get my information pack out of the safe.

I had started to use the safe by this point, after what happened the day before I didn't care if it blew me or everyone up as things couldn't get any worse.

It turned out the safe was SAFE after all! Yay!

I was locking my notes away as I didn't want anyone to see I was kicking up a fuss and get into any more trouble than I already had.

There were a lot of notice boards around the ward. When I was out and about I started to take in some of the information on them without looking like I had a short-term memory or couldn't read. If I'd had my phone I would have taken pictures and made videos, even though I wasn't allowed to do this. I make lots of videos online and I am very used to sharing my life journey publicly, as you can see from this book.

Anyway I didn't have a phone or any kind of device at this point just a good old biro pen and hopefully some more paper soon!

There was a very colourful poster with all colours of the rainbow which kept attracting me, it was a wheel of lesser minority religions. (I think this is how you would describe it, no offence meant!)

I remember thinking I had to choose a religion whilst I was there. Jehovah's Witness wasn't on the poster, I remember seeing Buddhism and pondered that as a choice as I am a very spiritual person, I like yoga and occasionally meditate, thing is I'm just not religious. My next choice would have been Rastafarian, I picked this possibility due to my dabbling in a little magical herb (marijuana) mainly for medicinal use but sometimes social too. Thing is I don't have the dreadlocks (I did when I was 18 and went to Trinidad and Tobago) plus I am a 40-year old white woman, not that it mattered, no discrimination here but I just wasn't sure I wanted to be forced to choose a religion.

I was called into the visiting room where my mum and dad were waiting for me. My chap wasn't due to visit until the evening as he had to work during the day. Had he known how important the meeting with the doctor was he would have been there. It was similar to the day before when we met with the psychologist, had he been in these meetings he could have vouched for me and explained what happened the week before.

I had the religious stuff on my mind and someone had mentioned intervention again, with a slight air of paranoia still lingering I wondered if this was my final chance to be saved!?!

Chapter 12

The Doctor

Mum and dad were clearly worried but they put their best brave face on as I cried and told them how awful it was and how scared I was. I reeled stuff off whilst pulling emoji faces at the people shuffling past the door and showed them the state of the 'Zen garden' through the perforated metal covered window.

"Look, it's awful it's covered in fag ends and it's a mess. Everywhere is a mess. What's going on? What have I done wrong? Why am I here?"

"The people here are so scary, I can't stay here. HELP ME!"

I tried to tell them what had happened the night before and showed them all the new bruises on my arms, I said I even have bruises on my inner thigh and all over my legs.

My mum looked so upset.

My dad said you'll be ok Liz. We can get you out, we will get through this.

I hoped he was right.

We were taken to see the doctor.

A man in a suit awaited. My dad said he looked like my uncle whom I thought had been in a bomb attack. What on earth!

He didn't seem like a friendly guy to me, I felt his air of presumption and could feel him judging me with his eyes. He had a job to do, once again he was doing his best, he must see so many different people doing his job. It was up to him to assess us all in a short period of time with some very outdated methods.

At this point I was the great unwashed, greasy frizzy hair which looked like it was falling out, old tracky bottoms my poor chap had grabbed in a rush and mismatched clothes. I must have looked like 'The Wreck Of The Hesperus', I bet I smelt pretty bad too. I had my notes though and I wanted answers.

It's funny as looking back this section of time was quite unclear but a few hours chatting to my mum once I was home brought back the memories and what follows was her funniest moment.

She said he asked me some really random questions. I answered them all ok and pulled a few more emoji faces for good measure. I was weird. It was freaking me out.

Then came the funny one considering what I'd just been doing outside the room. Maybe I was psychic, my intuition was strong on this day.

He asked me what religion I was.

I took a deep breath.

I clearly stated in a very firm voice that I don't follow any religious beliefs but that I follow my own truth and speak my own truth!

A few more confusing questions later I took my information pack and pen and asked what religion he was.

He said "I am asking the questions Elizabeth".

I ignored him and queried why my form had the wrong date on, six weeks from admission. He apologised and said it must have been a mistake, more care should have been taken, this was one of the things which freaked me out big time. Yes in future please be more careful, these are very important pieces of information especially for people who've had a breakdown and feel lost, alone, afraid, confused, helpless and out of control.

I also told him in no uncertain terms that I did not want the ECT electric shock treatment which was barbaric and I could not believe this method was still in use. I'm sure he said I didn't need to worry about that and mumbled something about using it for broken hearts. WHAT?

I was conscious my heart felt broken being in here but I didn't say it out loud just in case he changed his mind.

He said I had made a huge improvement from the woman I was the night before, the staff had filled him in on my raving amongst other things.

The mixed up medications had obviously worn off by then so clearly I had started to feel more like myself!

He said he was sure I would be out soon.

How soon? What was the procedure?

I didn't feel I could ask any questions, he'd already told me he was the one asking the questions today. Maybe I would get to see him again tomorrow and would be able to go home and see my fur family. As well as my dog Milo, I also have two cats called Levi and Lloyd and my amazing chap, comfy bed, beautiful views, countryside walks and all that good stuff.

I didn't want to think too much about all of this whilst with the doctor as the tears would have started again and this might affect my score rating on the 'is this woman sane or insane' paperwork!

I think I was being recorded too, there appeared to be some kind of machine behind him.

To be honest I thought I was being recorded or watched wherever I went in this place.

Observation?

At this point I felt it the right thing to also state that in case I was injured on the ward or worse still stabbed I would like to be clear that I would have a blood transfusion as I was not a Jehovah's Witness. I had also written a signed declaration on my sectioning form to say this too including my full name, DOB and a note saying I Elizabeth Green do declare I will have a blood transfusion if required.

You can get a feel for how scared I had been having to think about taking measures like this.

I knew that really out of control situations had happened on the ward, I could feel it in my bones.

Time with the doctor was and still is vague, I was simply doing my best to be the most sane version of what normal is to a doctor in a mental hospital.

In my day to day 'normal' life I connect with the everyday magic of life and love to chat lots, to people and sometimes even trees too! I sing my own song and play by my own rules. I am one of the 'Crazy Ones', just like I mentioned earlier on the Apple advert back in the 90s!

'Here's to the crazy ones.

The misfits.

The rebels.

The troublemakers.

The round pegs in the square holes.

The ones who see things differently.

They're not fond of rules.

And they have no respect for the status quo.

You can quote them, disagree with them, glorify or vilify them.

About the only thing you can't do is ignore them.

Because they change things.

They push the human race forward.

And while some may see them as the crazy ones, we see genius.

Because the people who are crazy enough to think they can change the world, are the ones who do.'

- Rob Siltanen

I didn't feel it was the best time to start quoting this poem, so kept my thoughts to myself but there was no way on earth I would be contained. I decided to keep taking notes and doing my own observation process.

Maybe, just maybe I could be one of the crazy ones who could change the world. The world of mental health circa 1983.

My dad was being his usual chatty friendly self with the doctor, I couldn't bring myself to be overly nice or wear any masks at this point. I just wanted it all to be over so I could find out when I could go home or at least go and get a nice cuppa tea.

The doctor didn't tell us anything, there was no information about procedures or how long I would be kept in there.

I think I went back into the visiting room with mum and dad for a short while after the meeting.

It was out of visiting hours so they had to go.

Mum had brought me a couple of her tops, a book I'd given her some time ago, Eat, Pray, Love. I thought back to the Saturday night when I watched Julia Roberts in the film Wonder and how I thought she might have been bombed along with all of the famous women who stood in their own personal power. I knew at this point that was not the case just my own paranoia and fears coming out of my broken brain.

Chapter 13 (Lucky For Some)

Back To Information Overload

My brain felt much better on day two. My emotions didn't but I always had the unicorns to colour in and some positive quotes to read.

I went back to my room and started to read the information pack again.

I cringed at the creepy picture on the first page and shook my head at the wording at the bottom which said 'With all of us in mind'. Really?

The first page talked about the ward, it said it was a 23-bed acute ward for working adults aged (18-65). Acute? Was I an acute mental patient? This totally freaked me out but I kept breathing deeply and read on.

The philosophy of care said care is service user focused (service user? Oh yes that was me). It said they identify the holistic need through use of nursing assessments and interventions. Holistic?

Holistic ~ Adjective:

'characterised by the treatment of the whole person, taking into account mental and social factors, rather than just the symptoms of a disease.'

For me the whole person is Mind, Body and Spirit. The therapies I am trained in and have experienced many times in the past are holistic, this experience was not. Everything was suppressed, fixed and pushed down with medication as not much else was available.

'Service users, relatives and carers are encouraged to actively participate in their care, ward routines and activities. Promoting empowerment is central to our philosophy. This is achieved by agreed care planning between key worker and service users, aiming to maximise independence balanced with appropriate nursing support.'

Really!?!

Empowerment!

The coaching I have offered in the past is called SHINE which stands for:

Support

Healing

Inspiration &

Natural

Empowerment

This was not an empowering situation to find yourself in. There was no encouragement to participate in anything, routine was a million miles away with staff changes and new faces every day.

The activities board was still on last week's dates so I decided to actively participate myself and the next time I walked past I wiped the date of Friday the 13th with a lick of my fingers and a swift swoosh. I'd told them again and again it had the wrong dates on.

Stuff like this made me feel very uncomfortable.

There was no agreed care planning, I took my tablets when I was told. In fairness most of the nurses were great and I totally get that this must be a very high demand high stress job to work in. A dear friend of mine is a nurse, I have always said the pressure for these kinds of jobs is too much and they don't get paid enough for the work they do. This is not my own version of a witch hunt, that's not my intention, I just simply want to tell the truth about how I really felt in there.

It was all a bit of a mishmash. Like Forest Gump said, life's like a box of chocolates you never knew what you were going to get next. These chocolates were definitely out of date though as they

THE DAY I GOT SECTIONED

never tasted any good to me!

'Our aim is to provide a safe environment which promotes psychological and emotional wellbeing, while providing privacy and dignity that encompass respect for the individuals cultural and religious beliefs.'

Safe? Some of the things I was told had happened on the ward in the past made my hair stand on end. I certainly didn't feel safe. Privacy seemed hard when someone was checking on me every 15 minutes and I didn't know what was happening. I felt I had started to act more dignified myself but it definitely wasn't a dignified place to be and being treated like a second class citizen or a child didn't feel much like dignity either.

I understand everyone in there has different requirements, stories and backgrounds but please don't put us all under a one-size-fits-all way of treatment.

The next bit spoke about the key worker again and how they take a multi-disciplinary approach to assist them to provide the best possible care.

No-one told me who my key worker was and I didn't feel very cared for most of my stay.

It also said that the service users representation is well established and participation in advocacy services is welcomed.

I realised that was what the guy I'd met before the doctor's

CHAPTER 13

assessment was doing, had I missed my chance for support?

I decided I would call the number of the advocate on the main notice board at some point to make sure I was legally covered for all of the queries and complaints I had already gathered.

The first page finished by saying that the nursing team accepts responsibility to liaise sensitively with family and carers whilst respecting individuals rights as service users.

There was a serious lack of liaison with both my chap and my family and friends who visited over the course of my stay. We were winging it!

On the next page was a paragraph about the Care Programme Approach which said I would be allocated a key worker, in brackets Primary Nurse, who would be responsible for working with me in planning my care whilst I was there. It took until the following weekend to get to know the nurses and who they were. It took until the Sunday to identify who my primary nurse was and fortunately she was lovely! Phew!

It turned out she lived quite near me so understood why I was missing home and the lovely countryside so much. More about that later, yes there is some good stuff to come too!

Let's get this shit out of the way first.

It said my key worker is also supported by other nurses, including nursing assistants, who work as part of my team.

I had a TEAM?!?!

Together

Everyone

Achieves

More

No-one ever discussed this with me. I didn't know who to go to for support especially in the early and most scariest days. I had managed to figure out who would help me and who was nice but wasn't aware of a team. It's such a shame this isn't made clearer and people didn't take a little time out in the first few days of my stay to explain how it would work because it didn't seem to work how this form said.

It did say I could request a copy of my plan, which I did but never got.

There was a rather large paragraph about what happens when you are discharged, this talked about community workers and therapy services. We will go onto that part later, I still had another eight days to survive and still hadn't even found the shower at this point and I was starting to smell. One of the other ladies stuck in there told me it took her two weeks to figure out where the showers were and how they worked! Terrible!

It said I could help them and myself by getting involved in my care, by taking part in the ward activities and meetings.

Apart from the doctors meetings and the advocates coming in for support, which was just a mishmash of people in the main area outside the office a few times a week, I was never told about any other ward activities or meetings happening or I would have been there in a heartbeat. Maybe because I was so scared and spent a lot of the first few days flitting between my room and tea top-ups I had missed something? It appeared not as nothing changed the week after.

They had a zero tolerance policy.

'The trust aims to provide you with a safe, therapeutic environment and will treat you at all times, with dignity and respect. Please treat staff with the same level of dignity and respect. Violence and aggression will not be tolerated, the police may be notified and their assistance called upon.'

The trust? I didn't trust the trust!

I wondered if I had appeared aggressive the night before. You see I'm 5ft 10 and quite well built so I imagined me singing, dancing and shouting at the top of my very loud voice was quite intimidating.

The thing is I was fucking terrified!

Anyway, that was then this is now. I had tried to apologise and would make sure I always chose my default setting of being pro peace, a peaceful warrior woman. Love and light all the way!

Where was that light at the end of the tunnel though and how quickly could I find it?

Activity information was on the next page, it said they were run seven days a week. It appeared there were a couple of things happening the week before as the whiteboard was still out of date, maybe they were activities, I couldn't read the writing. No-one made me aware of any activities, I was never asked to take part in anything or told about activities.

It said there were ward based activity workers and group or individual one to one sessions. Wow! One to one support? I would have loved some one to one support or therapy but there didn't appear to be anything to me. It was non-existent throughout my stay! I also wondered how I would get any exercise in this awful place. Maybe I had to wander around the 'Zen garden' a few hundred times to make up for my two hours of dog walking I was used to.

'Staff and activity workers will come and ask you if you want to take part in any of the sessions running that day. It is your personal choice if you want to join them or not but it is an ideal opportunity for you to socialise with fellow service users. The groups mainly run in a multi-purpose activity room or a fully equipped gym.'

There was a gym?

I've never been a fan of gyms, I prefer the great outdoors but had it ever been open I may have considered a walk on a machine instead. I never saw it in use.

I figured the 'multi-purpose activity room' must have been where I got the unicorn book and pens, it was like a very small classroom you experienced at infant school but the chairs were bigger.

It's so sad that I was never invited to any sessions (if there were any sessions that is). I am a joiner and love to take part in group activities and meet other people, this never happened and from what I could see we were each left to our own devices that week.

There was a little more about Advocacy and what an advocate did.

It said there were amenities such as vending machines, a cash point, shop and cafeteria in the main hospital as well as several shops and newsagents in the local area. I never got to see these as I wasn't allowed out. I knew the ward was in a bad area so that would have been too much of a challenge anyway for the anxiety filled state I now found myself in.

On the next page it talked about banned items, saying we must abide by ward rules, no-one who was in there or who visited was allowed the following items at anytime and if I felt I had any items with me which were banned I must speak to a member of staff.

Basically it listed anything which could cause harm. Cigarette

THE DAY I GOT SECTIONED

lighters were banned too but everyone was smoking, how were they lighting their fags?

It said if I saw anything banned on the ward I should tell staff.

I queried the lighters and the smoking but was told that they could not be controlled. I wonder what other banned items people have with them?

Scary stuff!

The next items on the agenda were Bathrooms, Bedrooms, Benefits and Beverages. I was sad to learn that sometimes nurses could lock the kitchen area so I may not be able to have my tea and that I wasn't really supposed to be having my own food brought in.

I missed out the child visiting section as I only have fur babies. Tears flowing again for the love I have for my furry family and how much I missed them. I wondered when I would see them again.

There was a list of controlled items which had to be locked up by staff and managed by risk assessment. This was things like razors or anything with a cutting edge, anything flammable and medication not prescribed by the trust's medical staff (I still had not got my Meniere's medication at this point and I knew the tablets I'd taken before admission would be wearing off).

Electrical equipment and flexes were mentioned which was such a shame as I was hoping to get something which I could play music on to drown out the noise and bring some much needed healing through music therapy of my own.

Once again they mentioned matches and lighters. HELLO! Has anyone been to the 'Zen garden' lately?

The last controlled item was vitamin compounds and herbal remedies which didn't make an ounce of sense to me as they were filling me with all kinds of nasty tablets. I knew my body was missing my herbal tablets I take each day which also help my balance.

There was a little bit about Drugs and Alcohol and some more on electrical items and how they had to be locked away when not in use. I didn't even have anything to tell the time on at this point let alone my phone or anything else to entertain me. To be honest I was shocked to see most of the other patients / service users / inmates were walking around on mobile phones and iPads. Maybe a break from the constant tsunami of information overload online might help them heal?

There was a section called Environment which talked about the ward's refurbishment back in 2011 (7 years prior to my stay) which was to make it a more welcoming and open environment. It explained the single sex lounges with their own TV and DVD player, neither of which I could get to work properly, there were three remotes none of which worked for either device, you had to twizzle the knob on the back of the TV to turn it down. I only know this because the news channel was playing constantly on full whack during my first few days stay which wasn't helping my anxiety.

Apparently there was a games room.

I'd noticed there was a football table in the main area but hadn't seen any sort of games room.

Up next, the beautiful outside area!

'Outside there is a therapeutic garden which has ornamental features, trees and shrubs'

(should that have said mental features rather than orna-mental!?!)

There was a huge net over the garden area, I'm guessing to stop the service users / inmates trying to do a runner, the place was a complete mess and some of the trees and features had been broken, scratched and carved into, hopefully not with any of the banned items or worse still knives!

Any trees in there were tiny little things which couldn't grow any higher than the net, it was the saddest little garden I've ever seen it made me cry.

I needed a rest from reading. This was all too much to take, it shocked me.

I went to get another top-up of tea and have a pee. I wondered when my chap would be coming. I decided I might go to the office and ask if I could call him but didn't feel I ought to as everyone else had their mobiles.

I sat by the window with my cuppa and did some colouring in and cried for a while. I could see people running around the corridors in the distance beyond the disused miniature football area.

I ate the sandwich my dad had made me which I had snuck into my room. It tasted like home from when I was a child. I cried some more.

Chapter 14

Crack On!

There was still a lot more information to go through so I thought I'd best crack on so I continued reading the documents.

It talked about Interactions with other patients (sorry I thought we were called service users?) It said if any of us had concerns we should speak to the staff. I had lots of concerns as I was still feeling paranoid about some people but thought it was just me and my crazy head. That wasn't always the case, I was confronted by a service user but more about that later on. The next part said there was an interpreting service.

Shame they didn't seem to be using it for the poor Chinese lady who was one of the service users who didn't seem to speak a word of English, bless her! Synchronistically enough my brother speaks fluent Chinese I wished I had learnt too, sometimes she looked so sad! Other times I saw her I said "Nihao" which means hello and she would laugh or smile at me. Bless her! She seemed like a sweet enough lady.

There was a designated laundry room and the rules were listed to ensure it be kept clean and tidy. I only had one encounter of the laundry room during my stay to try and retrieve my missing clothes from the first night, it was a mess, water all over the floor, broken washing machine and cupboards filled to the brim with other people's lost clothing.

I think it was one of the nurses who accompanied me to this particular room as I had been asking about my missing clothes. We didn't really talk and mostly communicated by pulling faces at each other.

I did a 'boggling eyes wide open' emoji face when she showed me inside one of the cupboards full of foisty old clothes. I turned to her with a 'what on earth is this mess' face and she just grimaced and shook her head giving me a wide-eyed 'it's totally out of control but there's nothing we can do about it' face.

I managed to find my clothes eventually, they had been washed within an inch of their lives and my jeans were about two sizes smaller. All good though as I lost lots of weight whilst on the ward!

Information about leaving the ward was up next, it talked about being escorted whilst off the ward and levels of observation which would be explained to me later on (they never were). It said if I was unsure I could discuss with my allocated nurse but I didn't know who that was.

It said when leaving overnight you had to take your belongings with you or have them locked away in the store room. I was sure if I ever got overnight leave from this place I would be on the next train to somewhere as far away as possible! Never to return!

Meal times were listed. Lunch and Teatime were protected meal times meaning it could not be interrupted by ward rounds, meetings or doctors visits. Shame I didn't see any ward rounds, meetings or doctors visits during my stay other than the 'once a week not worth the paper it's written on' assessment. I thought it was strange they used the word protected. Meal times were approximate and would usually involve someone knocking on my door, shouting to let me know or a queue forming outside the canteen.

Medication times were listed, 8am, 12pm, 5pm and 8pm and a note to say if you were prescribed medication at any of these times to please be around the ward. I wasn't told anything about my medication or doses so floated around the store cupboard style medication room at these times just in case.

I was being given medication four times a day to start with and had to ask for sleeping tablets on this day, due to the night time sirens, noise and lights being shone into my room. It was only the second night I'd stayed in this place, without help I'm certain I would not have slept.

The paragraph on mobile phones said they were at the discretion of the nurse in charge (who was that?) and should be used in your bedroom or quiet areas of the ward, there were rarely any quiet areas.

'On no account should mobile phones be used to take photographs or videos anywhere in the unit'.

I get this for other people's privacy but had I had my mobile phone I would have been taking some undercover detective photos and videos to show other people exactly what was happening on this ward. My chap knows me well, good job he kept it at home. Plus I didn't feel I needed any more information overload or to be connected to the outside world too much as I may have said something I regretted later.

Like a random 'Ferris Bueller' style Facebook post saying "FREE LIZ GREEN" or maybe even a live video saying "HELP ME!!! I AM TRAPPED IN THIS HELL ON EARTH!! NO-ONE IS LISTENING TO ME!! FREE LIZ!!"

There was a payphone in a private booth which I experienced earlier that day but I couldn't use it as I didn't have any money.

Observation:

'Upon admission you will be given a level of observation which determines if you can go off the ward. Everybody has different levels of observation so one may wonder why one can go off the ward when others can't.'

Yes one did wonder this (said in a posh voice).

'Levels of observation are reviewed by doctors and nurses to decide whether the level should be increased or decreased. A doctor or nurse should keep you informed of your level of observation and any changes made.'

Nope, they never did.

WARNING:

If you ever find yourself in a mental hospital situation please try not to be alarmed that during the night strange faces will appear at your door window and shine a very bright torch into your face every fifteen minutes to check you are still alive!

Hence the sleeping tablets required that night!

It also said I could speak to my nurse about occupational therapy, shame I didn't know who my nurse was!

There were notes about the pharmacy, postal address, religious and spiritual care.

My spirit was feeling pretty crushed at this point, I wasn't sure what kind of spiritual care they could give which would help.

I prayed.

ANGELS PLEASE BE WITH ME, SUPPORT ME THROUGH THIS LIVING NIGHTMARE!

Then came the smoking policy which obviously wasn't working

out very well.

'The trust operates a no smoking policy. This means that staff and visitors cannot smoke anywhere within the trust's buildings, grounds and / or assets. Electronic cigarettes / vaporizers are NOT permitted in hospital grounds.'

Followed by a note about how smoke free can help you quit.

I was a reformed smoker and had celebrated being smoke free for some time. That didn't last.

I would never have expected the reason for starting smoking again would have been because everyone else in the hospital was doing it and I felt like an alien going out to the garden for some fresh air. There's more to come on this but what a real shame that this happened!

Special diets were catered for but on the few occasions I asked for something meat free all they had was jacket potatoes and salad. I didn't eat a lot of meat and had been vegetarian for some time before going in.

Treatments were mentioned again.

'The ward offers a wide range of treatments and various approaches to providing treatment. Treatments you may receive maybe in the form of medication, group activities, one to one talking etc. Your treatment will be explained to you by a nurse or doctor.'

Wide range of treatments?

I only received medication to numb me down. Or make me high when mixed up!

We already know about the non-existent group activities, one to ones, etc....

I wonder what the etceteras were?

Maybe a few staff were on holiday the week I was in there? Surely it wasn't like this all of the time?

Nearly there!

Valuables, Visiting and Ward rounds were the last three points.

I didn't have any valuables, well just my mind, body and spirit which was already broken, bruised and crushed at this point.

Visiting times were listed again. I was so grateful that I had such supportive friends and family to keep me going and of course my chap! I really do feel for people in there without anyone and can see how people end up like my new neighbour stuck for thirty odd years!

The ward information said I would be invited to ward rounds and be seen by the in-patient consultant, never met him or her. It said I could ask family members to be at the ward rounds which were supposed to be on Mondays, Tuesdays and Thursdays but I never got to know the time of them so was ill prepared for what unfolded on the Thursday and never experienced anything other than a quick hello from someone on the Monday and Tuesday I was there the week after. What a load of rubbish!

'Your key worker or associate nurse will spend time with you in the days before ward rounds discussing the things you want to talk about. Towards the end of your stay in hospital you will have a pre-discharge ward round which your family and care coordinators (ermmm my chap?) will be invited to attend'.

Nope. This didn't happen either.

This information wasn't even worth the paper it was printed on. Total utter rubbish!

There was also a very blunt and poorly written list of 'House Rules' listing all the do's and don'ts of the ward and how its service users should behave.

I wasn't just a service user.

I was a person with a heart and soul.

Eventually some people started to see this thank goodness!

Going back over this information and sharing what happened from my perspective is bringing up a lot for healing, mainly frustration and deep sadness with the whole situation and how it's left me feeling back in the 'real world'. A little anger is popping in to say hello too, how on earth do they get away with this?

I'm surprised my tear ducts haven't packed in!

I'm also suffering with horrendous headaches since leaving the ward, as well as flashbacks and nightmares. Most of which I never experienced in my life pre-sectioning.

Then comes all of the anxiety and panic I have been left with, my confidence about life has been severely affected.

Sad emoji face....

Chapter 15

On A Mission To Nowhere

My chap was visiting soon, I was really looking forward to seeing him but also nervous and edgy about what I needed to tell him. I couldn't keep quiet and say everything was ok, it was far from ok.

I felt like I was on a mission.

Then I saw their mission.

The ward's mission and values statement:

> 'The trust has a mission and set of values that guide us in delivering high quality care to everyone.

> **Our Mission:**

> Enabling people to reach their full potential and live well in their community.

Our Values:

- Honest, open and transparent

- Respectful

- Person first and in the centre

- Improve and be outstanding

- Relevant today, ready for tomorrow

- Families and carers matter

Our values reflect the openness and transparency of the organisation.'

Don't even get me started on this!

There was also a few paragraphs about their aim which covered off lots of the points I had already read in the main document. It spoke about empowerment again and all the wonderful support and care on offer to assist my swift recovery.

I didn't trust the trust's information even on day two, by the time I had spent 10 days in this place and being weaned off the horrible medication I knew what I was seeing and experiencing was real and I would say for the most part the mission statement was a load of old rubbish.

Let me be honest, open and transparent, it was the ward which sent me over a deeper edge of breakdown.

Respectfully this was not a 'person first and in the centre' kind of place, the central theme seemed to be numbing everyone down as much as possible and fire fighting the issues when they occurred.

I'm not sure when they chose to improve and be outstanding and would certainly never use that word in relation to what I experienced.

Relevant today, ready for tomorrow?!?

REALLY? Maybe back in 1983.

Families and carers did not matter and it appeared that neither did I most of the time.

Job done!

My mission was clear. I would become a mixture of Miss Marple and Erin Brockovich and I would take note of everything, eyes wide open.

There was no way on earth this could ever be called a place of healing, I knew it was going to take me a long time to recover from this.

I decided to put the information pack back in my safe as I'd read all I needed to know and once again will say this much - it definitely wasn't worth the paper it was printed on! I wouldn't even wrap my fish and chips in it!

I had asked my mum and dad to bring me some magazines even

though I don't read glossy magazines anymore and haven't for years. You will usually find me at the hairdressers reading an inspirational or self-help book. I didn't have anything else to do so decided to have a flick through them.

They'd brought me a bumper pack of three women's magazines. As I started to leaf through the pages I was shocked at the articles which were featured and wished I hadn't asked for them. I wanted to get rid of them but continued to read them as I didn't have anything else to do.

The synchronicities were beyond freaky and made me feel those deep pangs of panic as if this was all a set up and someone was playing games with me.

Was this a test to see how well I could cope?

I started to do my deep breathing techniques I learnt at yoga. Maybe you should take a nice deep breath now too.

You see, I am into some very unique things one of which is a new business I had been setting up selling crystals for women to wear, called Yoni Shine. Yoni is the Sanskrit word for Vagina, I know I bet you thought it couldn't get any stranger! Some would say I make no wonder I ended up where I did, not the case as the crystals have helped me so. I am pro crystal and had worn Yoni eggs for the last year or so, they supported me, they helped me stay balanced.

One of the articles in the magazine was about Gwyneth Paltrow selling her version of these crystal eggs and how wrong it was that women were wearing them. Another article was about vaginas and started off with a letter: 'Dear Vagina - um fanny, toot-toot, tupence - we've been through an awful lot together, you dearest va-jay-jay are a fierce fanny force to be reckoned with.' WHAT?!?

One talked about women sticking crystals and tea tree oil up their bits and bobs and questioned these weird and wacky techniques.

Was this all directed at me?

Were these magazines fake, was I being filmed for some insider programme or was this a test?

Was this something else I was doing wrong?

I recalled that the week before my breakdown I had seen a guy from way back when in my past. We decided to connect online and he had checked out my Yoni Shine page. He messaged about the eggs and asked if I did Yoni Massage for other women (which I don't bTW, each to their own but I prefer to do my own). Not that I ever felt remotely sexual or sensual during this whole mental hospital experience, URGH! Anyway, this guy from my past was also a policeman, I wondered if he had he reported me for my spiritual Ann Summers escapades, was this a set-up?

I was still feeling paranoid!

There was also an article about sweat lodges which is one of the other spiritual practices I have taken part in the past. It was sharing a story I had read years ago when I researched if it was safe, why did the magazines seem so aligned with me and what was happening?

Then I came across another story about the dark side of personal development which talked about retreats where participants go for days or even weeks without sleep and are then initiated into a cult type environment and appear to have 'gone mad'. Is this what happened with my friend? I remembered her trying to hypnotise me and doing lots of weird stuff the week prior to my breakdown.

I shook my head in disbelief as I read on. The magazines felt so masculine, even though they were meant for women there was nothing soft or inviting about them, they felt bitchy and unsupportive. I circled a few of the articles and added a few notes to question if they were real or if I was being set-up. Paranoia kicking in again.

There was an article about OCD entitled 'My mind convinced me I was a villain' eek! Was the tattooed OCD guy a villain?

Another article was about digital dating and showed a picture of a cartoon man taking a photo of his penis which reminded me of the cyber flashing incident.

One talked about imaginary friends and said it's one of the first signs of madness. I love talking to the angels and my spirit guides, maybe this was one of the factors of my own 'madness'?

I did find a few useful things in the magazines like self-care for social media which made me feel relieved I didn't have my phone or internet as that was also a big part of what tipped me over the edge. On the cover of one of them it said 'Death by social media'. I decided not to read them anymore as they weren't helping my state of mind.

I decided to take a nap, my brain was aching too much.

It was so good to see my chap later that day, we cried lots and hugged harder than we had ever hugged before. He had brought me a beautiful little journal with a parrot on which said the following on the first page:

'For my lovely Liz. A book for you to write all of your good stuff.'

I knew what I would be using this for! Miss Marple notes! He had also brought me my new rainbow pen my dog walking friend had bought me a few weeks before.

I now had the perfect place for my detective notes and anything else I felt would be useful to write down.

He had also brought me our old iPod with some of my favourite music on, I was so happy and knew that being able to drown out all the awful noises would support my healing process.

He brought the charger too but I remembered from all of the paperwork that I wasn't allowed it in my room. It was fully charged for now so I decided I would worry about that later. Main thing was I had a pen, a notepad and some music!

He had also been and bought me a new phone without internet on so I didn't get overwhelmed again. It was one of those 90s style Nokia's which didn't even have predictive text set up but at least I would have contact with the outside world and a way to make calls in private from my room.

I was starting to feel a tiny little bit better, unfortunately he couldn't get the phone to work, and had the wrong earphones for the iPod, my lifelines were gone for that day. I was really fed-up and frustrated and took it out on him!

In the past we have rarely spent more than a night or two apart, we are a unit and do almost everything together. This was a real struggle and my chap came to see me every day no matter what.

My best friend from our village came this day too, I was trying to go through all of the information pack and explain none of it was true and that I didn't feel cared for. I said I had bruises all over me including on my inner thighs and that I couldn't bare to stay in this place.

I may not have shown my appreciation on this day as I was still so scared and paranoid but I was so grateful they stood by me and came to see me.

No music.

No phone.

All I had were those awful magazines or the choice of a few newspapers dotted about the ward which all seemed to be talking about Ant from BGT apologising for what he had done. This made me question the previous weekend's fears and consider that what I felt may have indeed been true. Had someone died after all? Was there a bombing?

My chap did bring me a couple of Paulo Coelho books so I decided I would try and read 'The Valkyries' which is about a group of powerful warrior biker chicks who live in the dessert. Trust him to bring me a book about motor biking, that's what he loves. I read the book on and off and it did give me a sense of reclaiming my own inner warrior woman at some point.

I went back to my room to cry some more once they had left. I experienced depths of sadness like never before. I felt so alone. I missed my life and didn't know if I would ever get it back again. I opened a tube of posh handcream my friend had brought me and rubbed it in to my dried up hands as I felt sorry for myself.

I set the intention I would do my best to start afresh the next day and try and get some of my issues resolved.

I started to write in my new notebook.

"Angels, please support me to get through this, protect me, wrap your wings around me and help me to get through this."

I also started to write the healing words of Ho'oponopono in my book.

"Please forgive me, I'm sorry, thank you, I love you."

I had learnt about this Hawaiian forgiveness technique a number of years ago. It was used by Dr Hew Len to heal a hospital full of mental patients who had some really serious illnesses. Without even seeing the patients he healed the full ward.

I was using the technique for my own healing and to do my best to bring in some better energies than I had experienced until this point.

"Please forgive me, I'm sorry, thank you, I love you."

I also started to write about how sacred I was and some of the things which seemed very off in this place.

I didn't know what would happen the next day but I knew I had my support team on the outside in place and they would be back to see me and hopefully support me through this.

I had the hope of the phone and some music coming too, I figured things could not get any worse.

I looked out of the window, beyond the metal and the dismal view and hoped I would see the moon appear from behind the clouds. I remembered it was new moon and thought back to the information I had read online.

I have followed the moon cycles for many years and understand that new moon is a time for huge shifts and can bring about significant changes in life. This particular moon aligned with a big shift which said it would change the course of humanity for the next eighty-four years.

I stared into the darkness for a long time that evening. I had another cuppa tea and ate some of the contraband food I had snuck into my room earlier.

As I mentioned before, this was the only evening I asked for sleeping tablets as the noise that night was too much.

I couldn't cope.

Chapter 16

Wonderful Wednesday?

A fresh new day a fresh new start? - Nope. Not really.

At least I had some shampoo and conditioner now and could try and figure out where the showers were. I had my pink ruffled sponge, my chap's overnight toiletries bag with a few essentials including my tea tree oil, if I dared to use it that was! I still felt a bit shocked about the article I'd read the previous day.

At this point I had thrush too, I know tmi but I believe our bodies manifest disease (dis....ease) based on what we are feeling, our emotions. This felt like the perfectly imperfect reflection of where I now found myself, in a very sticky situation!

There was no way I was asking any of the staff for help with this problem, I would use my trustworthy tea tree oil which always helped me sort these kind of things naturally. First I had to find the shower.

Thank goodness I had a few weeks before my next period, I knew this as I was cycling with the full moon. I prayed I would be out by then.

One of the doors near my room said toilet and shower on it. I entered the room and could only see a toilet, a sink and a plastic stool. Where was the shower?

I tried another 'toilet shower room'.

I couldn't find the shower and there was no way I was going to use the electrocution bath!

I think it was about half past 7 and I knew I had to hurry up as breakfast was at 8am, they would be coming to get me if I wasn't ready.

I remembered the wet room the man in the shirt and tie had shown me the day before. It looked a little like what you would expect a small gas chamber to look like, I gulped a big intake of detergent filled air and opened the door to the shower room.

There was a big red button and a big blue button on the wall. I knew this was for hot and cold now and had let go of The Matrix film analogies. I looked around for somewhere to put my colourful stripy beach towel wishing I was on a beach right now. There was nowhere to put my stuff and keep it dry but at least I could get clean. I stripped off and started to shower conscious that faces kept passing the window and thankful it appeared to have privacy glass, at least I think it did.

I showered as quickly as I could feeling my body sweating as I rushed about so as not to be late for breakfast and have someone come and collect me before I could get dressed and sort myself out.

The hot water didn't stay on for long so I kept pressing the red button as I cried about the flashbacks I was experiencing.

I returned to my room and got dressed as quickly as possible. I tried to squeeze into my shrunken jeans but they were way too tight, I needed to allow space for deep breaths so chose to wear a pair of old leggings which were in my grey bag.

I cleansed my face and used some of the lovely moisturiser my mum had brought me. I was conscious that the infection control leaflet said I should not keep any items which had been open for longer than a day or two. I pushed all of my cosmetic items to the back of the top shelf and put things in front of them so that nothing would be confiscated. Plus I didn't want to get into trouble for anything.

Mum had brought me a cloth tote bag so I popped a few essentials in there like my book, my rainbow pen, the unicorn colouring book, felt tip pens and my new notepad.

I decided to have breakfast with my nose in my book and then go and do some more investigating. I could feel my strength returning.

I had to be strong.

I CAN and I WILL get through this.

After breakfast I decided to venture outside. As everyone smoked and shuffled around me, I felt out of place and wanted to fit in. I thought about starting smoking again to help me get through this time.

There was a really tall very stocky old guy outside F~ing and blinding throwing various things around the garden. He shouted out the C U Next Tuesday word, was he shouting that at me?

I went back inside.

Lots of other people shuffled slowly past me, he followed me inside. I thought I'd be safest sat on the green plastic sofa in the main area outside the staff office. Surely if he attacked me they would do something.

Another lady was there she looked kind but had really sad eyes, as did I. We sheepishly gave each other a tiny sideways glance and a small smile. I liked her but could feel our joint sadness.

I put my bag on the floor and tried to bury my head in my book as I started to say my healing mantras in my head.

He was coming towards us.

He fronted up to me, stood on my bag then moved sideways onto my bare toes popping out of my flip flops. OUCH! That hurt!

He threw a fag in my face and shouted some more profanities at me. I felt it could get a lot worse than this. What should I do?

The lady next to me started to cry.

I could feel tears welling up.

Stay strong Liz!

A very shaky but lovely guy who was also a service user told him to back off and treat us women with respect.

The staff came out after what seemed like far too much time had elapsed and tried to reason with him. I went back to my room to recover and cry some more.

I needed to smoke.

A nurse popped in to see me and check I was ok. Wow! Someone came to see me!

I wondered if you had to be in a dangerous situation before you got this kind of treatment but I hoped not.

I was told that if anything else like that happened again I should shout "HELP" as loudly as possible or let someone know I wasn't safe.

I knew I wasn't safe and was still telling everyone this anyway but no-one was listening so what was the point! I guess I was like the girl who cried wolf by this time, the thing was I didn't feel SAFE, far from it!

I told the lady, who I think was a nurse, that I needed to start smoking again as that seemed to be the only reason people went into the garden. I'd said I would get a bin bag and gloves and clean it myself but was told there was no point. She told me not to start smoking again and to get a vape stick. I wanted to smoke.

No-one was coming until later on.

I thought about asking my chap about it.

I ventured into the TV room on this day, I didn't want to watch TV but I had noticed there was a different view from the window from there. I tried to change the TV channel to something other than the news. None of the remotes were working still. I unplugged it and turned it off. I sat in the window and did my best to focus on the view, my book or my cup of tea.

The tears kept welling up.

Stay strong Liz!

After this day I spent the first part of most mornings sitting in this window and looking at the trees outside. I missed my walks in nature. I missed my dog, magical Milo the doodly labradoodle (yes that's his full name). I missed my views. I missed the alpacas, chickens and sheep in the field next to my lovely little garden but if I talked about my views and the alpacas in particular people seemed to think I was making it all up, at least I think that's why the staff rolled their eyes so much.

I was thankful I could see a few birds on the trees, I opened the window so I could hear them too. Tears bubbling up by now as I did my best to suck in some fresh air through the metal cover.

I thought I could see a duck pond in the distance, I wondered where I was in relation to the area and felt I needed to get my bearings, I would ask my mum and dad exactly where we were as this would help me feel more grounded.

I felt like I was on an aeroplane, taking a never ending flight to nowhereville.

A lady joined me in the TV room. I'd seen her around the ward, she didn't want to be there either. I didn't want to appear nosy so tried not to ask questions, in my previous life back home I was super chatty and loved to make new friends and chat to people wherever I went, as I said I am a very sociable girl! I had no-one to talk to in here, I was so alone.

I felt sad when I saw the lady's outfit, why didn't someone help her?

She was rather large with low hanging and rather big boobs (no offence meant I am just saying it how it was). Unfortunately her top was shorter than her boobs so they hung out of the bottom. Bless her soul!

I felt so sad for her. She made me smile though, she told me I would be ok. I decided to go back to my room and try to process everything I was feeling.

I wasn't sure how I should be interacting with the others. I wanted to be nice and polite and make friends but I wasn't sure what had happened to people and didn't want to trigger anyone.

I ripped the message off my herbal tea bag.

'Spread the light, be the light, feel the light.'

I wish!

I now had a growing pile of tea tags with their sweet little messages building up on my windowsill. I never closed my window in room 21, I needed to allow all of these dark, dense and tense feelings a way to leave.

The weather had been really strange again. On the week which led up to my breakdown it was freezing and thick with fog, I could usually see my village on the top of the hill from my friend's kitchen window. I had been stuck in a dense fog all week. I had felt separated from my normal life, out on a limb. As I mentioned before, the weekend of the actual breakdown it was cold with thick fog on a morning then overly warm on an afternoon, I'm certain I wasn't the only one who found it confusing. No-one knew what to wear and at this point I had the smallest capsule wardrobe ever!

Hot cold. Hot cold.

I drifted through the day. I told staff about my concerns, no-one listened, nothing changed.

Someone would be here to see me soon.

I decided to put some towels on the floor in my room and did some yoga. It helped me feel more balance and start to process my emotions in a more balanced way. Thank goodness for yoga!

I wondered why they didn't offer yoga classes in the ward as it would really help people.

What a shame.

I also decided to do some 'Sylvester Stallone, Rocky' style press-ups and get my strength up in case the stocky old guy fronted up to me again. I needed to protect myself no matter what!

My yoga friend visited that afternoon. She brought me a yoga mat and some print outs of the yoga mudras as well as the softest most beautiful fleecy blanket I had ever seen. She brought me some homemade lemon drizzle cake too, I wasn't allowed to eat anything in the visiting room but knew I would enjoy it later on. We hugged, I cried and took a few deep breaths.

Thank goodness for friends and for yoga!

I thought back to the last yoga class which I had missed and how I couldn't stop crying about the situation with the friend whom I was looking after.

I had been so out of my routine and all of those wonderful things I had set in place to keep me balanced and healthy. I knew yoga would help me and hopefully I would have some music soon too!

Three days before my breakdown it was my yoga friend who had been to see me so I could chat to her about what happened the week before, she only lived across the road. She listened and held space as did many of my other friends but I think I was too far gone by that point.

Anyway here we were in the visiting room together, I told her about lots of things which were worrying me but felt much calmer this day. Those evil tablets had worn off and the towel yoga and press-ups had helped.

I showed her the 'Zen garden' and the shuffling people. I was still doing slight emoji faces to try and express my concerns. She got it!

We chatted lots, it was lovely.

My mum and dad came too. They seemed happier to see that I was becoming more of the Liz they once knew and loved only a short time ago.

My chap came.

He had the phone and it worked! BINGO!

He had the iPod and that worked too!

Yessssss!

Things were starting to feel more supportive.

I felt so sorry for the people in there who didn't have this kind of loving support from outside, how did they cope? I make no wonder people were trying to harm or kill themselves in this place.

I was still very unsettled at this point, asking when I would be able to leave but no-one was getting any answers, it wasn't just me who became a number in the system, everyone was being kept in the dark.

My chap had brought me a gift as well as my other lifelines. A magical little bracelet called a Wish String. It was a simple black thread with a little silver star on it, behind it was a picture of a rainbow and some hearts and stars. He told me he had seen a rainbow that day too over the field at the back of our cottage. I always took rainbows as a good sign, even when it rains the sun can shine too and create such a wonderful sight.

I mustered up a smile as he gave me this amazing and very thoughtful gift. The message on the packaging said tie it five times and make a wish each time you tie a knot and when the string breaks your wishes will come true. Obviously we were both wishing for me to be back home but I wondered how long it would take for the string to break.

I made a few other wishes about my comfort and safety as well as having more support and friendly faces around me. BTW I am still wearing the Wish String today, it hasn't broken yet but my wish of freedom came true!

He also brought me some more clothes and books I had requested as well as my crystals. I wasn't sure if I would wear them in here, I'm sure if I got found out that would just add to the medical opinions of me not being of sound mind. Mum and dad had brought me a lovely little spring plant so I popped the plant pot next to my growing pile of inspirational tea tag quotes and the rainbow card from the Wish String on my windowsill.

I spent most of the evening in my room, I also had my angel cards now too so didn't feel as crazy speaking with my angels whilst listening to some of my favourite tunes on the iPod most of which made me cry buckets so I sobbed and let it all up and out.

I started to send a few messages to my friends and family who had visited. It took ages texting letter by letter but I didn't mind as it passed the time. I also called some of my friends to tell them what was happening and how horrible it was.

Thanks to the phone I also knew what time it was which helped me to feel more grounded too.

The craving for outside space and smoking also kicked in big time this evening. I would have to ask someone for a cigarette, who would I choose? Definitely not the old stocky guy he was far too much of a loose cannon.

There was a young guy who had smiling eyes, we had done a little sideways smile at each other a few times, he felt like the right person to ask.

I did a bit of angry yoga to some heavy metal music (never done that before!), I also did some more press-ups to get my confidence and strength up. I decided to travel around listening to my music to make it easier to keep myself to myself. I took my tote bag and angel cards so I could look busy in the 'Zen garden'.

He was out there having a fag.

I looked over and caught his eye, he smiled, I cried a little but managed to hold it together enough to ask if I could possibly pinch a cigarette, I offered him chocolate or crisps in exchange, he was lovely and said it didn't matter, it was ok. He lit my newly acquired fag and told me it was a menthol which pleased me as I don't really like the taste of normal cigarettes, does anyone?

I sat on a bench at the furthest point away from old stocky guy who was throwing apples at people and swearing again. I smoked and pretended to look at my angel cards. The smoke made me feel dizzy but I stuck with it and felt more like I fitted in, plus it was something to do. I was really ashamed but also sad that I started to smoke again as I loved being smoke free and still couldn't believe this temptation was pushed in my face in what was supposed to be a place of healing.

I went back to my room for a bit and cried about the smoking thing until I needed another.

I phoned my chap and told him he must bring tobacco and a lighter the following day. I told him I missed him and added a few other things for him to bring. He was my rock!

I ventured out to find more fags.

There was a tall woman who was probably quite a bit younger than me and reminded me of one of those confident friends many of us knew from school, she walked with a powerful stride, she was passing my room as I opened the door. She was the one who told me it took her two weeks to find the shower room, bless her!

I asked her a favour, I said I really needed to smoke as this place had really got to me, tears welling up again, I said I had crisps and chocolate, she said it didn't matter and gave me two fags, bless her!

I knew she knew. She felt my pain.

All I had to find now was a lighter. That wouldn't be hard, I just had to ask the right person and stay safe. I managed to light the last two cigarettes, got more tea and went back to my room.

I sent some more text messages. Once again it took me ages to type the messages letter by letter but I didn't mind as it kept me occupied. I also asked my spiritual friend to copy and paste the new moon reading offline and send me the details. Bad move!

The phone could only handle a few short messages at a time and filled up fast meaning I had to start deleting important messages from my chap and my mum and dad.

PHONE STORAGE FULL.

This went on for a few hours as I tried to read the copy and pasted messages which were all coming through in the wrong order.

CLEAR, CANCEL, DELETE!

Even this felt frantic and after counting nine hundred and sixty three messages later about the bloody moon I switched the phone off and locked it in my safe.

ENOUGH ALREADY!

My chap had also brought me an eye mask to block out the flashlight night checks, it was one I bought him years ago as a joke and said 'does my nose look big in this' on it. This didn't even make me laugh anymore, this was no joke!

I chose some soothing chakra balancing music on full whack and went to sleep with my iPod. I woke up with said iPod stuck to my cheek the following morning.

Chapter 17

Transformational Thursday?

Transformations? Nope. Not really!
Nothing on the ward had magically transformed but I did feel a little better this day as I had my music and lots more of my stuff around me which helped.

My phone meant I knew what time it was which was nice, I got up at 7.30am for a shower.

I decided I would make sure no-one was watching me and wear my amethyst crystal, yes in my fanny, foo-foo or whatever you choose to call it. There was nothing sexual about this process, as I said before I didn't feel remotely sexual, sensual or any other flavour of this kind whilst on the ward or for quite a while after leaving it for that matter. I was still feeling deep shame and a little self-loathing for good measure. I missed my magical baths, they always helped me to feel better no matter what life threw at me.

This was a very different kind of ball game.

THE DAY I GOT SECTIONED

Amethyst is my birth stone so I set the intention I would keep the faith and look forward to my rebirth back into the world at some point. I had no idea when this would be.

I hid the crystal in my toiletry bag along with a few showering essentials and went to the wet room hoping no-one would be about. I cried some more as the water washed over me, releasing, cleansing and clearing what was ready to go. I popped the crystal in with a few drops of tea tree oil and felt an inkling of my personal power return.

Breakfast now consisted of two slices of wholemeal toast with margarine and jam. I had the same each day as I had vowed not to touch the cooked food again since the Monday and had been living on the sandwiches brought in from the outside world. Some of these were from our local health food deli shop and they were one of the highlights of my day. Even better if I managed to eat them in my room like I did the night before when I also had a gluten free ginger and chocolate Tiffin. Even though I had to stuff it all down pretty fast so as not to be caught it still tasted delish!

Breakfast also consisted of avoiding any of the unsafe service users. Having my music, books and angel cards helped me to keep busy and multi-task during these times.

I enjoyed my morning routine of sitting in the TV room window and looking out at the trees. On this day I saw a squirrel and thought back to the previous Saturday when I went to visit my neighbour and friend to try and explain what I had been through with our mutual friend and that sectioning nightmare. Maybe the squirrel would give me a wave?

I craved nature.

I craved hugs.

I craved support of some kind.

The trees and my new hospital squirrel friend would have to do for now. I opened the window so I could hear the birds and switched my music off for a bit whilst big fat tears rolled down my cheeks.

I yearned to be back out in nature!

I missed Milo and fur baby cuddles. I missed the smell of my fur family and wondered if I would be out to see all the spring flowers.

Outside some of the staff were congregating around the back of an outbuilding, maybe they were going there to have a smoke? I would be able to smoke again later on that day.

Apparently today was one of the days the ward rounds happen. I didn't see any rounds and once again no-one came to see me or told me anything other than when the canteen was open and when medications were being dished out. I'm not really sure how the tablets made me feel and thought it must have only been a low dose of 5mg of diazepam but I was told at a later date that it was quite a high dose.

The music and yoga helped me relax more.

Writing did too.

'Dear angels, great spirit please support me to navigate through this very strange situation, I have no idea how it all happened and I am doing my best to piece together all of the missing information. I was simply doing my best and this has turned into a complete nightmare!

I am only taking a small amount of medication, so I am ok, maybe I've just got to go with the flow and get on with it?

I just want to be back home with Cat (Ian), Milo, Levi and Lloyd I love them and miss them all so much.

I miss my beautiful views and the alpacas, I miss my home comforts, it's Ian's birthday next week and we have a wonderful trip away planned to Chester I was looking forward to it so very much. I feel so sad. I just want to get back to my normal life.

Dearest angels, great spirit, guides of the highest good please support me to rebuild my life.'

The ward started to get really busy again, people everywhere. What was going on?

I told them the whiteboard still had the previous week's information on (minus Friday the 13th which I had wiped off myself), nothing was updated, no-one told me anything.

Go with the flow Liz.

A lady approached me and said she was the advocate in a hushed voice. She asked if I would like to go to the canteen for a chat, I thought this was a good idea and I already had my notes with me.

We spoke in undertones, I was conscious of all of the people around me, other service users and staff, I didn't want to get into trouble for kicking up a fuss about everything as I thought they might keep me in longer.

I asked the advocate if it was safe for me to go through this information and if she was safe. She assured me it was ok, she seemed on edge but I wondered if that was just the environment, she seemed a little like me, I trusted her.

I started to share some of the stuff which was going off and how unsupported I felt, she said she could help me. I said I needed to get home, I needed to get out of this place ASAP.

As I didn't feel overly comfortable speaking with her in a such a busy environment I didn't say too much. She said her colleague had seen me on Tuesday and told her how scared I was.

ARE YOU SAFE?

AM I SAFE?

IS THIS PLACE SAFE?

She said I seemed more relaxed. Well as relaxed as I could be.

After her visit it was lunchtime so I knocked on the office door and asked if I could have some of my food out of the fridge as I had saved a fruit box and sandwich from the previous day.

As the information pack said it wasn't recommended that food be brought from outside and I felt like a burden most times I asked for my food, sometimes they would roll their eyes at me depending upon who I asked, other times it was ok and a friendly face would help me get my food.

The canteen was so busy! Full of new faces, I think some of the people in there were visitors and staff this day but I wasn't sure.

I ate as fast as I could, hid my face in my book and returned to my room as fast as I could with my cup of tea in hand.

I felt overwhelmed by what was going off around me so decided to stay in my room until visiting time. My vampretic craving for nicotine had also returned at this point too so I did some more unicorn colouring, sent some text messages and tried to distract myself.

I chose eight pens in as many different colours as possible and popped out to return the pen box to the 'Therapy room', maybe there would be a kind face to chat to in there? Plus I didn't want to get into trouble for taking the full box of pens to my room, I was also conscious someone else may be in need of some colour therapy.

It was a short visit, the tattooed guy was reading the paper and didn't say much at all. The service user who defended me the previous day was in there having what looked like a panic attack, he was shaking so much his red hot tea was going all over the place. I asked him if he wanted to take some deep breaths with me as I could feel panic setting in too.

I looked at him and said Breathe, Relax, and Allow. We can do this!

BREATHE. RELAX. ALLOW.

On the outside world and in my first book, 'Connect With Your Inner Truth & Everyday Magic' this is one of the techniques I love to use and call it our BRA!

Breathe

Relax

Allow

He seemed a lot calmer and stopped spilling the burning tea all over himself. I felt good for sharing this kind of support, it helped me too. I love to help others and he'd helped me the day before when the old stocky guy fronted up to me.

There was nothing else happening in there and I didn't feel comfortable or very supported by anyone else so I returned to my room without a view.

Visiting time was a welcome break in the day. I was really looking forward to seeing everyone.

I had more notes to share too!

So that's what I did.

More hugs, tears, squeezes and reassurance.

Another Wish String!

This time it was a Buddha, we did the tying ritual and made our wishes.

We talked.

I shared my shit.

I was given bags of goodies with food and my requests were fulfilled.

I felt the love and shared the love.

I said sorry and thank you lots.

I had tobacco now too and my very own lighter hidden in a

supermarket bag amongst the food.

Ironically enough a few days earlier my chap brought me my dressing gown which had a lighter in the pocket from lighting my incense at home. I had handed it into the staff as I knew we weren't allowed them but this was before I realised what was really going off! Funnily enough there was also a crystal skull in my dressing gown pocket too, I'd been hiding this in my bra so I didn't get into trouble!

I didn't want to rush my visits but I was craving a smoke so felt a bit happier than I usually did as I left the visiting room and was left to my own devices again.

I felt more confident now I had an excuse to go outside to the smoking garden maybe I would feel like less of an outsider.

Smoking that evening gave me more chances to smile at the service users I had already briefly connected with, this made me cry too!

I was sure my tear ducts would break at some point but they didn't.

I decided to have toast before my medication that evening and a few fags too. I had pre-rolled a handful of cigarettes and put all the smoking contraband away in the safe so no-one took it off me and I didn't get marked down for any rule breaking.

I started to walk with my head held slightly higher. I felt like

I was starting to remember who the nurses were. There were some earth angels on that ward, they must have such a hard job. I didn't want to make their jobs any harder, I did what I was told and even though I held my head slightly higher I still kept my head down and went with this very unnatural flow as much as I could.

I sat in my chair in the window and saw a slight glimmer of the first part of the crescent moon and prayed to the angels that I wouldn't be in there for full moon. I cried some more thinking about my chap's birthday in a week's time. I had only ordered him one small gift online and he chose that, a Levi's shirt. I hadn't even got him a card and there was no way I could go visiting a big city after all of this stress and anxiety. Our mini break was ruined!

I knew it was going to take time to get over all of this. I wasn't sure if I would be out anyway. I was certain I wouldn't be in there years like some of the people but still wasn't sure what would happen or what was even wrong with me.

I put my iPod on shuffle as I received and sent messages cried some more and drunk tea. Each time I went to top my tea up I went for a smoke and looked at the stars through the netting.

I would get out. I could get through this!

I called my chap to tell him how much I loved him and how much I missed him, he let me talk to Milo and Levi and Lloyd, I hoped no-one was listening as I didn't want to be the crazy cat or crazy dog lady. I felt so sad!

My iPod seemed to be psychic and played all my favourite songs with meaning, I cried myself to sleep and slept ok in between the nightmares and bright lights shining in my room as I chose not to wear the 'does my nose look big in this' eye mask anymore as it annoyed me. My checks were much less frequent, that must have been a good sign!

Chapter 18

Fabulous Friday?

Fabulous? Nope. Not really. No day could ever be fabulous in this place! Unless it's the day you are leaving and even then it's mostly anxiety which is felt!

I felt upset that I would be trapped in this place on a weekend. My weekends were usually spent visiting local beauty spots, walking, talking, seeing friends, watching films and some good series on Netflix.

When it was chilly we would light our real fire and I always loved lighting my candles and incense.

At least I was having a detox from wine though!

I was losing lots of weight too!

I didn't really care about all of this though, I just wanted to go home.

Breakfast.

Cup of tea by the window in the TV room.

Music. Reading. Tea runs. Smoking.

The occasional smile from someone or sometimes even a little chat. I knew I was being observed but still craved more contact, more support and someone to tell me what was going off.

In the background my chap was trying to get me some time out that weekend. He knew I wanted to see Magical Milo and if he could have brought Levi and Lloyd in a cat carrier I am sure he would have done that too.

Animal Therapy is an amazing way to heal, he knew how much this would help me.

No-one kept him or anyone else in any kind of loop, a serious lack of communication which was nothing like the 'Mission Statement'.

I was looking forward to the weekend as I knew visiting times were increased so I would have more support.

The days started to meld together with the same routines, I had a few new things added into the mix today. I wasn't allowed a razor but my best friend had brought me some waxing strips, I had my make-up now too so decided to kill some time with a little waxing and make-up.

I felt someone was watching me through my door as I stood in my underwear and attempted to wax my legs and armpits for the first time ever. OUCH!

I did my best not to scream out as I didn't want anyone thinking I was losing it again!

O U C H !

Someone was watching me, I saw a face at my door window and threw one of my best "get lost and give me some privacy" faces I could muster.

There were two guys who I think were agency staff on the ward who gave me the creeps. I didn't trust them and certainly did not feel cared for by them.

Maybe they were just looking at my tattoo?

Waxing done I looked at myself in the plastic mirror on the wall doing my best to ignore the slight fun house hall of mirrors effect they had on my face making it slightly wider than usual.

I had loads of spots. It must have been the medication. I squeezed a few and felt a little relief in the pain, I squeezed a few more and dabbed some tea tree oil on my face.

I had washed my hair that morning too and decided to wear a love heart vest top as it was warm weather. Maybe the love hearts would help me to feel better.

I think this was also the day that I had a rebellious moment and decided to draw some love hearts and a rainbow on my door name tag. I hadn't had a name for the best part of the week, so it was lovely to see someone had written Liz on it!

Were they noticing me?

Would I get some more support?

I'm sure the love hearts and rainbows gave a few people further opportunity to do eye-rolls but I didn't care. This was me!

I am who I am and I will be what I will be!

I smoked. Drank tea. Read. Looked out of the TV room window at the trees. Looked out of my window at the awful view. Listened to music and wondered how everyone back home was going?

The day dragged on. I did my best.

I took a nap. I'd had lots of sleep and definitely caught up on any I missed the week before. I was shocked Friday 13th was a whole week ago and spent a lot of time going back over things. At least the whiteboard had been updated now and they had written Liz in brackets next to my Sunday name Elizabeth on the other whiteboard which said who my nurse was. I didn't really know who anyone was still so that didn't help but let's be thankful for small miracles hey!

As I said, I was starting to recognise a few familiar faces and felt there were a few nurses or staff members who cared.

Behind the scenes my chap was still frantically trying to get me some time off the ward. He knew I needed to see Milo and have some time in nature.

He was making calls to try and speak to the doctor who had seen me earlier in the week to arrange some outings and also make sense of why I hadn't had any other medical follow ups.

I had slept loads, got over the earlier mix-up with medication which tripped me out again and apart from being in such a dismal place I was feeling stronger and more mentally balanced each day.

He had to chase and chase.

The doctor was unavailable so he had to speak to his understudy, conversations were had with the nurses.

Funnily enough on the Friday afternoon I saw the doctor who'd assessed me earlier in the week. I felt hopeful when I saw him and knew if I could have a chat with him I would be able to express how much more of myself I was feeling. I could explain how I was ok to go home or at least get some time out of this hospital prison.

I shouted his name, he looked distracted and said he was busy and could not speak to me, he put a spurt on and rushed off, he was nearly running to get away from me or at least this is how it felt!

It's so wrong that you only get one doctors assessment a week and that determines how your whole week goes. Thank goodness for my rock! He brought with him good news, another Wish String and some nice food too!

He had managed to arrange for 4 x 15 minute outings over the coming weekend.

It felt strange to be told that I was allowed out but only for such a short period of time. Was I really that bad that I could only have an hour outside of this place split into such small sections of time meaning I wouldn't really be able to go anywhere other than the hospital grounds? I knew it was in a really crap area too with no countryside or nature nurture anywhere nearby.

Why were they doing this to me?

Why was I being treated like this?

He said he would bring Milo and mum and dad on the Sunday, this way someone would be able to wait with the dog whilst we were inside.

I WAS GOING TO SEE MY FUR BOY! YAY!

This gave me a huge boost!

Today's Wish String was a spiritual hand, maybe it would give me a helping hand in here? I didn't say anything at the time but it was the same little silver hand I had used to adorn a piece of wood wrapped in rainbow thread which we used to use for our Women's Wisdom Powwows, we called it a talking stick, we did the talking not the stick!

I missed conversations, I missed my heartwarming chats, I missed having the spiritual support I was used to. I was used to opening up and speaking from my heart, my soul and my inner spirit all of which now felt like they had been squashed out of me. These gatherings were also something I did with my friend whom I'd had all the issues with during the lead up to my breakdown which brought up another layer of sadness. Since the unfolding of everything which happened, and for my own self preservation, I have had to cut ties with said friend which is such a shame but I've had to trust my inner guidance on this one.

That evening I ebbed and flowed between pissed off, frustrated, some anger towards my treatment and a tiny sprinkling of hope about my outings.

BTW I have never been an angry or shouty person and often find it hard to deal with any anger, usually not even bothering to feel it, bottling it up and slipping into tears and sadness as I don't like confrontation or arguments of any kind. I have always been pro peace and continued to be this way on the ward. Apart from the first night in there I never raised my voice or actually said very much at all. I was as polite, kind, gentle and quiet as I could be always saying my pleases and thank yous.

I missed my Friday night wine, TV and all the other simple home comforts. At least I had my music and my fags! I'd had one of my sandwiches for tea and I had some chocolate too, my friends would be visiting over the weekend as well.

I knew I would get through it, I had to.

No-one else was going to do it for me!

But it was so hard.

The stark realisation that I was held prisoner on this ward and no-one could do anything about it until the following Tuesday when I would be given chance to meet with the doctor again.

Why didn't they do an assessment every few days? My main issue was lack of sleep, I had slept. Psychological damage had been done since then as I was now stuck in a really horrible place and I was smoking again, at least I was having a detox from the weekend wine though!

There was no Friday night TV for me, the remotes didn't work anyway so I chose to keep myself to myself and stayed in my room as usual with the occasional trip out for a tea top-up or a fag.

I'd had an iPod upgrade on this day, my chap had managed to get me an old iPod which had more storage and uploaded our full library of songs from iTunes so at least I had my 7000 and odd songs to keep me going. I still had to ask staff to take me to the store room for my iPod charging but did my best to time it when I had visitors. One time the lady helping me nearly took me into the seclusion room and laughed as she said "Ooooo you don't want to go back in there now do you?!" NOT FUNNY! It made me feel very anxious!

The iPod seemed to play to my moods again, lots of love songs, sad songs and songs about regrets. Songs which reminded me of certain holidays, songs which reminded me of gigs and festivals we'd been to. I healed through the synchronicity of whatever played next and went to sleep as early as I could.

Chapter 19

A Lovely Weekend Trip Out?

L ovely? Nope, not really. This place had never seen a lovely
weekend trip out that's for sure!

I didn't know what to wear and the weather was going from hot
to cold again. I did have a couple of dresses but might be too
chilly. I didn't want to look too overdone or wear something that
didn't fit in conscious that a strappy dress may offend some of the
different ethnic backgrounds of the men on the ward.

I opted for my dark blue jeans which I did most days, turned up
a little at the bottom and worn with my purple Doc Marten boots
to help me feel a little bit tougher!

It had taken my chap a few days to get my boots to me so I had
been wearing slippers the first couple of days then flip flops. It felt
good to have sturdy outdoor boots on.

I missed my wellies and I missed the grass and mud too!

I didn't want to wear my purple walking coat he'd brought me as it made me feel too sad as it reminded me of all of the magical walks I was missing out on. I kept opting for the dark blue hooded cardigan which I was wearing when I was admitted, sometimes my big comfy shawl thrown over for good measure or warmth when the sun dipped behind the hospital buildings out in the smokers garden.

I had some hand-knitted rainbow socks in there with me too which usually stayed in my attic room at home for comfy warm Shamanic drumming sessions or meditation. When I was feeling more confident about being myself I would wear them with my flip flops. Socks and flip flops are never a good look but I thought I may as well embrace the crazy stuff now!

Shower, Toast, Tea and a fag.

I made sure I always showered before breakfast and only left my room in my dressing gown later on a night as I didn't want them to mark me down for moping around in my dressing gown and slippers.

I got dressed and felt comfortable with my chosen outfit for my first trip out.

Visiting was all day on the weekends, I clearly remember my trips outside but the time seemed to morph during the rest of visiting times in between food and cups of tea.

My second trip outside on the Sunday was the most memorable. The police were there and security had to be called but not for me this time thank goodness! More about that in a little bit.

As I've already mentioned this Priest themed ward was not in a very nice area. In fact it was a really awful area I would never have chosen to visit.

I remember feeling really confused about going outside, not knowing what to expect.

I struggled to find my bearings and didn't know where we would go. I had already asked my visitors where the ward was so I had an idea of the bus and driving routes people would take, once again not a very nice drive to this area either.

The nurse had to write on a whiteboard near the entrance to say how long I was going out for and where we were going. Apparently we were going to the bench, rock n roll!

We had to go through a few sets of security doors which were locked, there were lots of people around, hustle and bustle.

I breathed deeply and stayed as strong as I could. I used one of my favourite mantras from the TV programme Friends, the one where Joey has given Chandler Rachel's stop smoking tapes (ironic). He listened to them whilst sleeping without realising they were for women.

"I am a strong, powerful and confident woman!"

"I am a strong, powerful and confident woman!"

It helped a little bit.

I didn't know which way was out. We headed towards some more doors, I could see outside!

I held back the tears as we stepped outside, there was a wooden bench with a table across the road. The lovely nurse said we could sit there for the 15 minutes, she seemed happy to be outside too!

My friends came that afternoon too. I think I kept popping back into the ward for tea and to smoke a little too but my memories are mainly on the visits outside so it's a bit of a blur. Each day was melding into one.

I craved being at home, Saturday night in here wasn't the kind of evening I would ever wish for!

I went straight back to my room to cry once everyone had left, this was my usual after visit emotional clear out. Today was more intense as I'd been out but not out in the way I would have liked.

My mind was racing again.

This had to stop!

I ate one of my sandwiches in the canteen. A few of the service users must have been out on a jolly, they came back with pizza and coffees. I glanced over longingly, they handed a piece of pizza to another one of the girls in there and she smiled, she obviously knew them and I thought that was really nice of them.

I went outside to smoke.

She was out there too, the sun was shining a little through the net sheeting over the outside area which made sure we couldn't get out.

My lighter had run out, I had already called my chap to say he MUST bring one the following day as I didn't want to have to ask people for a light in case something bad happened!

She smiled so I asked her for a light.

She told me my make-up looked lovely, I didn't have any make-up on as I'd been crying so took it off. I thanked her anyway and saw how beautiful she was, in a really natural way. She was only young so didn't need make-up anyway, I told her she looked lovely too and how nice her hair was. She shook her head and told me she had tried to set her hair on fire the night before as she lit my cigarette. I wanted to cry.

WHY THE FUCK DID WE HAVE LIGHTERS IN HERE?

I felt ashamed as I was part of the smoking club now too, but this was serious stuff! I had to say something to her, she had to know she was an amazing and beautiful young woman.

I said "don't do that lovely, you are beautiful!"

I gave her my best smile right from the centre of my heart and beaming healing, love, light and all of those magical things I once beamed around like they were going out of fashion.

From that moment on whenever I saw her I made sure I always gave her a smile, she always gave me one back.

I felt what others were feeling in this place.

I have always been really sensitive and picked up on other people's feelings and emotions, this added to my own healing as we were all thrown in this awful mix together. I felt relieved that I was able to keep myself to myself most of the time yet the paradox was I really missed the company.

I went back to my room for a cry.

A nurse came to see me that evening too, I think they must have realised how alone I had felt. As I had shared more about the build-up to my breakdown they wanted to help me.

I really appreciated this support.

This was definitely not my ideal way to spend a Saturday evening. I had seen some copies of films in the TV room but there was no way I was going to try and get the DVD player to work or figure out how to change channels.

Medication, toast, tea and a fag.

I asked the nice young lad who'd given me the cigarette during my moment of weakness the previous week for a light, he smiled which made me want to cry, he was so polite and said it's ok and moved along swiftly giving me my space.

I did my angel cards and read my book whilst listening to music outside for a bit.

I started to feel sleepy.

Early to bed early to rise.

As I said the weekend is a bit of a blur, I got two out of my four outings with my chap and parents on the Saturday, alongside a nurse keeping check. I ate some food, took some tablets, read, smoked and listened to music. I think this was the day I decided to listen to some heavy metal music again to try and clear my frustrated angry vibes. The power was off first thing Sunday morning so no-one got their toast and the large lady with the low hanging boobs was annoyed the TV wasn't working.

I did collect another two more Wish Strings over the course of the weekend and loved those moments with my chap, I had started to smile more with him and didn't cry as much as we tied them on and made our wishes together.

I found it difficult to think about what I was going to wish for, I thought about life being easier than it was before I was sent to this place as money had been tight and my chap's business was still relatively new. I made a few wishes and thought about being back home.

The first Wish String was a dinosaur which made me laugh, I guess that represented my old outdated prehistoric habits, patterns and cycles which were ready for recycling.

The second Wish String was a dog, how wonderful that I got to see my dog this weekend too. I tied it around my ankle as my wrists were filling up.

Talking of dogs, I knew Milo would be coming on the Sunday and I didn't want to break down in tears. I had to be strong as there would be people around, I didn't want to make a scene.

My mum and dad came again too, my chap went to get Milo when the nurse came to get us.

My chap was running from the car park with Milo, his little paws were going ten to the dozen as my chap ran with him. Ohhhhh my! I had missed him so much, my doodle pop! Labradoodles are often used as therapy dogs so I knew he would help my healing process too, shame I couldn't go for a lovely walk with him somewhere familiar but at least I got to smell his fur again and tickle his chin.

He was so excited to see me he started to jump up, I didn't want him to fuss too much as I recalled the issues the weekend before and how my dancing and him jumping up got me into even more trouble. I bent down and gave him the biggest squeeze ever! His tail wagged more than I've ever seen it wag before.

Then he just settled down into being Milo and we sat at the bench. It felt really unnatural to be sat outside the hospital with a nurse watching over us. She sat on the other bench but I could feel the time ticking away and worried about it running out, I did my best to enjoy the time out but it was hard. I just wanted to go home away from this horrible place.

It was time to go back in.

It had gone too fast.

Oh well maybe I'll get to take the other three outings soon. I knew my chap would make sure of this! If it hadn't been for him I wouldn't have got any of these, we had to keep chasing them up to make sure we got them too! Over the course of the weekend I didn't get to take all of the outings but after what happened on the second Sunday outing I didn't really care.

It was time for our second Sunday outing.

We were with the nurse I felt I was getting to know, the one who didn't live too far away from me on the outside world. She was really kind and between her and a couple of other nurses I felt I knew the earth angels of the ward that weekend and over the days which followed.

I even started to open up a little bit more and briefly shared

THE DAY I GOT SECTIONED

where I lived and the gorgeous views I missed from my garden including my alpaca friends and this time they believed me and asked me more about where I lived.

This time we got to stay out a little longer, I asked if we could visit the duck pond I could see from the TV room in the distance. It was actually more like a large puddle with a few reeds in it, located next to a housing estate round the corner from the hospital entrance.

As we headed out of the hospital entrance my chap looked worried, I walked ahead with Milo, my dad kept looking back and hurried my mum along.

What was going off?

I didn't feel very safe here and not in a mental way like the weekend before, this time I actually felt like we could quite possibly be in danger, actual outside world danger.

There was a man with some sort of crowbar and walkie talkie in his hand chasing two other guys, lots of shouting and threatening behaviour, some kind of kerfuffle!

WHAT ON EARTH WAS GOING OFF!

My chap said "we need to get out of here it looks like some kind of riot might start!"

The nurse called security then a police car arrived, we kept moving towards the 'duck pond'.

I walked a little bit faster, much faster than the walking we did on the ward. I didn't look back with Milo in hand on his lead. We walked past the duck pond and back around to the ward.

Well that was nice!

What a fantastic afternoon outing that was thank you very much! Worst nature nurture session I've ever experienced in my life! I wasn't sure if I wanted to go out again!

Maybe I was safer inside?

It's a good job my paranoia had settled and that I was feeling much more myself except for the awful tablets they gave me. Had I been in a similar state to that which I was in at the beginning of the week I think this would have been the point where I passed out or spontaneously combusted!

Back on the ward and safe we looked around in disbelief. The nurse had gone and we were all left to chat about what happened.

They must be used to this kind of stuff but we certainly weren't.

PLEASE TAKE ME HOME!

I WANNA GO HOME!

I genuinely felt I could not take any more, it wasn't a suicidal feeling as I was grateful to be alive and that all my loved ones were alive too. It was a feeling of emptiness and stuckness. Like there was nothing I could do but ride this awful wave until it came crashing down on my head and pummelled me into the rocks below.

My visitors left for the day. I went back to my usual routines and on my way for tea and a fag one of the nurses, who I didn't really know, said we could go for a walk out.

I wasn't prepared as I'd slipped my flip-flops on over my rainbow socks and said I would look silly or crazy. She was nice, she chuckled and said it would be ok. I hoped there wouldn't be any more trouble outside and went with the flow. We took a stroll to the 'duck pond' and sat on a bench, she asked me what had happened, I said it would take too long to explain the whole story. I chose to tell her about what had happened the previous week and how I hadn't slept for days, the tears started to fall and she gave me a much needed hug. I asked if it was ok for me to talk about these kinds of things, she said it was good to talk, I agreed.

It felt good to open up and start to clear the air, I wished there had been more of this kind of support. I couldn't understand why there wasn't, this is the most important kind of healing, rather than suppression of emotions via medication. Yes the medication can help but it's a balance between the two, practical medication as well as human interaction, love, support and of course HUGS!

We had to get back as the 15 minutes went so fast, she came back to my room with me and gave me another hug. I was so grateful for the support.

I wondered why I hadn't had very much support before or any one to one sessions or time to share what happened in a supportive and healing environment.

The main focus seemed to be medication based but I knew this would just suppress the feelings within. It would all come up and out in time but I knew this was going to take a huge amount of healing.

Chapter 20

A Fresh New Week A Fresh New Start?

Monday wasn't very magical but I held hope that something would change when the follow up with the doctor happened on Tuesday. Maybe it would be transformational?

I think the phlebotomists came back on the Monday, they looked normal now but I still didn't want my blood taking. No-one had told me to starve myself, which meant they couldn't take my bloods, so I had a lucky escape because I had eaten one of my daily sandwiches.

Staff had changed again, a familiar face was back from the week before and the night of my freak out, it was the slimming world nurse (aka potential friend). I didn't really know her but she was an earth angel and always smiled even when she was rushing about.

Sometimes I would see her trying to calm people down and try and get them to feel as normal as possible.

I went for my first medication of the week and she asked how I was, I told her I had been outside at the weekend but only for a very short period of time. I asked what she had been up to at the weekend. She said she had been on a retreat, I loved retreats!

It was really synchronistic, she told me they had done Reiki and alternative therapies. I told her I was trained in Reiki and loved all things alternative as well as shamanic drumming and quickly told her about my visit to Peru before the next person came in for their medication.

I wanted to ask her why there were no therapies in here and explain more about myself and what I loved but there was no time. Plus it felt weird that a week ago on this day I had the biggest freak out ever and still felt like a fool, like I was stupid. She wasn't the one making me feel this way, I was still beating myself up about all the stuff I did.

She gave me one of her nice smiles and we said what a small world it was.

Oh how I would have loved to have been on a retreat, somewhere magical to help me recover from all I had experienced. It was too late for that. The damage was done. I wasn't even sure if I wanted to do anything spiritual again and after all of this couldn't even imagine having my confidence back to take part in anything like this.

I went outside to smoke and think about past retreats and magical things I had experienced in my life.

Would I ever feel this way again?

Could life feel magical again?

I wasn't sure.

The lovely nurse who lived locally to me on the outside world came to see me later that day to say she wanted my section to be lifted and that she would do all she could. It was confirmed I was due to see the doctor the next day. I think she was my primary nurse.

She spoke to me about not rushing things and that if the section was lifted I could choose to stay as a voluntary patient which made me feel confused as I had spent so much time saying I wanted to go but felt really unsettled about that becoming my reality. How would I cope in the outside world?

What would I say to people I knew?

How would people treat me?

What would people think of me?

It was a paradox.

A push me pull you energy. I tried not to over think things and explained that I would like to be out for my chap's birthday on the Thursday but didn't feel up to the trip away. I was aiming for

Thursday and had asked my chap if we could go for a lovely long walk to one of our favourite places in the Peak District, Hope Valley. I felt nervous but hopeful.

I told her I had a gift to wrap up for him and had asked him to bring it in later that day. I also wanted to make him a card and asked if there was somewhere I could do that. She said the 'Therapy room' had stuff like this.

Shame the ward didn't have therapies too!

My Wish String that day was an elephant, we tied it to my other ankle and made some more wishes.

I felt like one of those circus elephants tied on a very short rope.

I wondered if any of my other wishes would come true. First things first the getting out of here wish we made last week.

As I write this here today none of the strings have broken yet but the main wish for freedom did come true!

I am open to other possibilities as I do my best to rebuild my life. More about that later on.

I spoke to my mum and dad on the phone this week and told them to take some time out and rest, I felt stronger and didn't want them to keep having to trail over to this hell hole.

My tea tag messages were starting to repeat themselves, a week ago today I was singing and dancing like a woman possessed, I laughed inside when I got the 'sing from your heart message' again.

I decided I would give it to a lovely young guy who seemed to walk faster than the other service users, he had a good energy and had given me a chocolate bar the day before when I was feeling sad. He didn't say anything, just a smile and chocolate bar bless him!

When I saw him I smiled and gave him the message, he said he'd better not sing or dance as that's what got him here in the first place! He'd been raving in the streets!

At least I wasn't the only one who'd been dancing in there.

He was sweet.

Maybe I was starting to see the sweetness in people as I was starting to feel the relief of the possibility of going home again but at the same time I had lots of angst about my return home too and how much of a fool I had made of myself as well as all the embarrassing things I had done.

I wish I could have spoken to someone about all of this but knew by now it was each to their own. I did have a lovely guy come and see me from another advocate service. I had called him the week before from the notice on the information board without realising he was from the wrong district, we live on the brink of two areas so I was confused about who was my advocate at the time.

I welcomed his soothing voice and half an hour in the visiting room with a caring person who asked me to tell them about what had happened, he also had tissues to wipe up my tears and I appreciated my time with him. At least I had the chance to release some of the stuff I'd had to bottle up.

The psychologist boy popped into my room at some point on this day too and asked how I was. It was a very brief chat, I said I felt much better for sleep but what a terrible place this was and how it hadn't helped but actually hindered my recovery. I didn't want to say too much in case he thought I was losing it again so hid a lot of my true feelings at this point.

I needed to get the assessment with the doctor out of the way.

Could the following day be the transformational Tuesday I was hoping for?

I slept well that night. I saw the moon from my window and looked forward to being back home on my evening stroll up the lane with Milo, I hoped my confidence would return.

The ward was really busy again the next morning. I made sure I was up nice and early to make myself look presentable and as sane as possible. The Liz before all of this madness loved to talk about the weird and wonderful. Now I had this rather harsh reality check I felt I had to be really grounded and as 'normal' as possible, whatever normal is.

Don't be weird Liz! Don't be wonderful Liz!

My chap had arranged to be with me for the assessment. As I mentioned before, it hadn't helped my situation that he wasn't there for the previous week's interrogation. Had he been with me beforehand he could have confirmed that I wasn't hearing voices in my head. He could have explained that the previous week's antics did actually happen, leading to the stress and lack of sleep which then caused my psychosis including all of the misunderstandings and misinformation of my knackered brain.

A familiar guy stopped me in the main area of the ward, I recognised him right away and knew his name, he was surprised I remembered and told me I wasn't in a good place a week ago, he said I was very scared. I knew exactly how I'd been acting previously, it was all stored in the filing cabinets of my mind, for processing. He said we could go to the visiting room, and that he was the advocate and was going to help me with the doctor's meeting. He mentioned his lovely colleague who I spoke to the week before and gave me a little more information about what they could help me with.

I asked him if I could raise all of my queries about the ward, the lack of support, organisation, care and all of the other anomalies I had experienced. He said I could but first of all we needed to get the doctor's bit out of the way.

He started to share some of the information about advocacy but I

THE DAY I GOT SECTIONED

could feel my mind getting overwhelmed again. I needed to stay calm and focus on the job at hand.

He said the doctor would ask me and my chap some questions and that he was likely to sign me off the section which would most probably end in a handshake and a goodbye.

A FUCKING HANDSHAKE AND A GOODBYE!

REALLY?

Job well done Liz!

You survived this ordeal!

See you later alligator! Hopefully not.....

It was a very surreal meeting. I remembered the room from the week before, it felt better now my chap was there and the nice advocate guy was there too giving me reassuring looks.

There was also another member of staff, I'm not sure what his role was but he was the 'sing from your heart' man who was in the seclusion room on the Monday night the week before. I still felt like a complete fruit loop in front of him and continued to apologise for my behavior.

I was starting to find it really hard to let go of anything.

The doctor was ok-ish to be fair, I'm sure he didn't mean to be the way he was, I'm hopeful he wasn't a bad guy, I hoped no-one was, as I've said before I'm sure everyone was doing their best within their job roles. Who knows everyone had their own agenda in all of this!

He said how well I was doing and what a transformation I had made. BINGO there was the transformational information I was waiting for although I made no wonder I was doing better now they'd stopped mixing my medications up.

BTW I didn't get my Meniere's medication until the last two days of my stay, the angels definitely supported me with my balance and I managed to get through all of this without a Meniere's episode! It was the last day when one of the nurses told me I couldn't take the anti-sickness tablet as it clashed with whatever they had been giving me. I was starting to piece things together.

The most memorable bits from the meeting with the doctor were the strange and somewhat archaic statements and questions.

He kept saying that me and my chap had been together for fifteen years so you could say we were as good as husband and wife, even though we are not married. We are strong in our relationship but don't need a piece of paper to prove it.

This time round he didn't mention religion, I am assuming that was because my mum and dad weren't with me for the second meeting. He related his questioning to my chap and talked about football of all things! Very sexist if I do say so myself!

My chap hates football too!

Apparently this particular doctor can err on the side of wrongness sometimes and has been known to ask race, sex or age related questions or statements. We got a football question and breathing exercise. Nice!

He asked my chap the 'Can we free Liz' question. He said something like this:

"If Liz was on your football team and she broke her leg would you as manager of the team say she was ready to return to the field and play again?"

He responded "YES of course I would" and the doctor asked for a percentage out of 100 to make sure I was definitely ok to play football again, he said 90% fit to play again!

Football? Please!

Were these kind of questions set in 1983 when this whole sectioning system was created?

Apparently this particular doctor is a stickler for his house rules and likes to run a tight ship. Personally I think it's wrong that people's lives and minds are left in the care of one person and the team below them. There should to be more procedures set in place to make sure wards are run with a patient focused caring manner, rather than service users who feel like they are just names on paperwork rather than actual people. Maybe someone should re-read the information pack and study up on the mission statement!

As I said before, I have a feeling this meeting was recorded on both occasions, I also feel lots of other stuff was recorded in there too! There were green flashing lights in some of the circular ceiling lamps, maybe they were motion sensors, maybe they were cameras? If anyone has the recordings please send them to me! I would like to listen and try to gain clarity about what actually happened. Here in the now, I can only share the parts I remember including my feelings and emotions which were stirred up and mixed like a crap cocktail at a shit party.

For the umpteenth time once again I apologise for any misinterpretations, it can happen to the best of us including the carers of us service users.

Then came the breathing exercise.

I was asked to count to 10, everyone else did it with me too. The clock was ticking rather loudly at one end of the small and now quite warm room. I have to give another HUGE SHOUT OUT to YOGA!

I calmly look a nice deep breath and closed my eyes, I relaxed my shoulders and connected with my breath. I practice Ujjayi breathing as part of my weekly yoga sessions and had been doing it regularly in my room to help me heal.

I took four lovely deep breaths, before I could make my way slowly to 10 the doctor stopped me.

"What did you get to Elizabeth?"

"four"

My chap got to 26, bless him.

The advocate was way past 10 as he was sat under the ticking clock, even the doctor looked surprised at this point.

He said the section would be lifted, he was signing me off the ward and back into real life.

Just like that.

Abracadabra!

The magical doctor wand had been waved.

Then came the handshake.

Oh yes, guffaw, guffaw, a nice firm handshake and well done Elizabeth. I felt like I was back in corporate.

I also felt anxiety.

Was this it? Right now?

I had to leave right away?

With no re-orientation into the real world?

I could feel my breathing speeding up.

I did some of my deep breathing and counted slowly in my head.

"Do I have to go right away?"

I hadn't packed.

I hadn't prepared.

In a whoosh and a handshake I was supposed to just leave and go back to my normal life after the last nine days of whatever I'd just experienced?

Would I get some support?

How would I deal with all the psychological disturbances I felt?

The worst of it all was created by this ward and my time there. Now they wanted to ship me off.

I was confused. I said I felt anxious about leaving right away and said one of the nurses told me I could stay a little while longer to get my head in the right place to return home and face everyone and try to rebuild my life which felt pretty much broken at this point.

I didn't feel like I could ask any questions, it felt so rushed, what would I do?

I knew I had a massage to come home to which my wonderful friend had bought me just before I lost it to try and help me relax.

She had also gifted us a two night break away somewhere nice.

I told my chap I couldn't go home. I needed to go on retreat, go and stay in our favourite cottage in the middle of the Yorkshire Dales where I wouldn't see any people for a week or so, this way I could reacclimatise and reintegrate back into my life.

I hadn't even called or text anyone to tell them.

I was still "Liz hospital" on most people's phones.

I wasn't ready for my old phone back either and the internet, I didn't feel I could cope with the world wide net!

All of that mess from before.

People to see.

Places to go.

Why didn't they let me have longer breaks out of the ward to help with this reintegration?

A total of about one hour and thirty minutes outside of the ward, during such a long period of time did not help. Plus I didn't get any visits home either!

The doctor said I could choose to stay as a voluntary patient. The nurse had already told me about this and said it would be a good idea to help me feel more balanced and give me a little time.

It's paradoxical.

I wanted out.

I so very desperately wanted to get out and now I could get out I wanted to stay in.

Once again bless my chap, he went along with whatever I felt was best for me. I decided that a two hour trip out that afternoon would be enough for me to cope with and said I would be out on his birthday for our trip to the Peaks.

This gave me time to try and process everything and create my own plan of returning home, no-one else was creating any reintegration plans for me so I relied on myself again! Steady does it Liz. This would also give me time to let everyone know using my hospital phone and to ask for space and time to heal.

Why didn't the medical professionals build this into the plan?

No-one even mentioned follow ups, support, counselling or such like. I felt like a sick little baby bird with broken wings being pushed out of a nest made of old rubbish.

I asked my chap not to say anything about the voluntary thing for now so I could work out how to handle everything without my brain feeling the pain again.

Chapter 21

A Trip Down Memory Lane

For my first two hour trip outside as a semi-free woman we went to Starbucks, my chap knew there was one nearby to where we used to live fifteen years ago but he didn't know the way. Some Sat Nav would have helped at this point. Even just walking to the car, seeing it and also sitting in the car felt weird, let alone being passenger.

I felt off balance, the world felt like it was on fast forward, after nine days of mostly zombie walking life felt intense. I stuck with the deep breathing and thanked my photographic memory for remembering the way, it turns out we could have taken a much more direct route but at least I knew where we were going.

We passed a guy just up the road from Starbucks dancing in the street, I asked my chap if he was real, he told me he was and that he should probably go to 'The Ward'.

I daren't go in Starbucks in case I had a panic attack or passed out, plus I was still on one or two of those tablets a day which left me feeling a little disconnected. I waited in the car semi-excited about my Venti Skinny Extra Hot Hazelnut Latte.

Tears bubbling up at the simplest of things.

How on earth was I going to get back to normal after all of this?

I asked if we could drive somewhere more rural. We chose a section of countryside road near an ice cream parlour and stopped near a field with some horses in and a nice view over the hills. Tears still bubbling up and some frustration too, I felt annoyed that my first trip out had been so complicated with all the directions and the drive through a shitty area.

I just wanted to be whisked away to some beautiful countryside retreat, I had forgotten about our very own little countryside retreat back home and only remembered the negative bits to start with. I was thinking back to what happened leading up to my detention in the ward and also facing up to what had happened and telling the truth to my friends and neighbours and the online world (eventually).

I am an open book, as you can see from this open book, I have to share my shit as well as the good stuff, I can't and won't wear a happy mask when life's hard and this was the hardest time of my life I'd ever experienced.

I'd taken my lunch with me too, an avocado and prawn salad

which I had before my coffee. We sat on a fence and had a smoke, the coffee tasted sweet but the thought of life didn't.

I kept telling my chap we needed to go away somewhere, he said we would be ok, that I would be ok and it would take time.

He was there for me one hundred percent and had been on his own healing journey whilst I was in the ward. He too had a lot of support from family and friends with people cooking for him, phone calls of support as well as a visit from one of my long standing friends whom I text whilst on the ward.

They didn't want to overload me with visitors but they were there for us both.

I breathed in the fresh countryside air once I'd finished my fag, once again gutted that I had started smoking! That was the least of my worries for now.

I had to get back to my life.

I knew it would never be the same again. I didn't feel the same, I felt this had somehow changed me forever.

We'd parked next to a huge pile of horse shit too which was very fitting.

Before my breakdown I was in the midst of writing my second book called 'Shitology' a play on words and a humorous book with a serious life intention behind it.

'When life throws you shit, turn it into manure and grow something beautiful!'

I wasn't sure how I could grow something beautiful from all of this recent shit but I knew I would get there. Once this book is complete I will be returning to 'Shitology' and completing that book too.

I breathed in the horse poop filled air and looked across the fields.

My chap hugged me. I held him, I felt the love. I was free, well nearly!

Now it was time to free myself from my own fears and worries, now it was time to start to rebuild my life.

A new life.

A new way of being.

I felt a little hope return as we returned to the ward. It felt different now I was there through choice, I didn't feel like I had to act a certain way or worry about being myself as I knew they wouldn't be able to keep me in or give me any of those nasty treatments like Electro Convulsive Therapy.

I still wasn't up for getting a bath in that place but I knew my return home and my chap's birthday was only a day away.

Only two sleeps to go! Actually it turned out to be only one sleep to go as things progressed.

We were conscious of time and didn't want to upset any apple carts by arriving back late so we made a move.

We got back to the ward and signed me back in.

I went back to my room when we returned and breathed a sigh of relief. This was it. I was a free woman, not yet free in my mind but free on paper.

The nice nurse, who I now assumed was my primary care worker, came to see me to chat about what I was going to do. She recommended that I go home the following day and spend the night at home before my chap's birthday as this way I would wake up with him too.

I felt so nervous!

I told her how I felt but she said I would be ok, there was no need for me to stay in. I said I would spend the full day on the ward and he could pick me up at 6pm on the Wednesday evening, this way I could have a day to pack my stuff up, wrap his present and make him a birthday card in the 'therapy room'. I would create some therapy of my own through artistic expression.

Yes this felt good.

A day to allow my energies to settle.

I felt like I had been on a huge flight into some strange parallel reality. An aeroplane to nowhere. No destination, just a very surreal ride with a ward full of people I didn't really know.

I only used to listen to music on headphones if I was flying anywhere in the past so this could have been the connection with the plane. I did feel rather off balance too and having music playing in my ears so much hadn't helped with the tinnitus but at least it was better than hearing all the commotion.

I called my chap to tell him the plan of action.

He was great, he went with the flow and said whatever I needed to feel ok.

He was booked to pick me up at 6pm the following evening, I had 24 hours left in this place, I would make it count and start to allow any emotions to come up and out which I was feeling about my return home. Obviously it wasn't as simple as that as emotions are complex as is the brain muscle.

I did my best though.

This was the most confident I had felt on the ward as I was now there by choice. I felt I could say more, have some conversations and be more myself.

There was no party.

There were no celebrations.

I didn't tell anyone about my freedom.

I just held space for myself and my inner knowing that I had and would get through all of this.

We were going to the countryside the day after next, that would be magical!

Beautiful views, fresh country air, my chap and magical Milo plus a stop at a darling little heritage cafe for latte and cream scones. I could feel the peace in that. I wasn't sure how I would feel on the Wednesday evening but we would cross that bridge when we came to it.

I slept soundly that evening.

They were also allowing me to take my herbal tablets for the Meniere's now too and let me take them to my room.

I had lots of crisps, nuts, dried fruit and other goodies to eat and drink before my departure, I planned to give them to the other service users the following day and share the love.

I also had enough herbal tea to quench the thirst of a small army by this point.

Tomorrow would be good deeds day.

I planned to get the energy moving in the right direction and do my best to create positive change.

It couldn't have got any worse that's for sure!

Chapter 22

The Last Morning

I felt different that morning when I woke up, I didn't rush to fit into their schedule and decided I would stay in my dressing gown for my toast, tea and morning fags then I would start to pack my things up.

I didn't feel like I had to prove myself anymore or be the good girl and stick to their rules.

I knew they couldn't keep me in now and I was feeling my rebellious freedom flowing.

Staying in my dressing gown for a few hours was about as rebellious as it got.

It turned out lots of people wanted to see me now I was leaving to make sure I was ok and I wished I had got ready earlier, I felt like a bit of a slob when the manager of the ward came to see me.

I didn't know who she was.

A nice but somewhat stressed lady knocked on my door and came in. She said I'd asked to see her.

I didn't know who she was or recognise her, I must have looked confused not that confused mattered in this place as it was most people's regular face.

She told me I'd asked for a meeting with her and that she was the ward manager.

I said I had asked to see her a full week ago!

I wanted to express all of my concerns about this place and share my notes along with my own personal experience of being a service user and experiencing this not very funny comedy of errors.

I felt annoyed but knew it wasn't her fault.

Whose fault was it?

A broken, out of date, under-funded system which was expected to survive and do its best.

I had to take some nice deep breaths at this point and remind myself that no-one was at fault in this whole process.

Everyone was doing their best.

Humans, perfectly imperfect.

I'm~perfect.

Far from perfect but I had to have empathy and understand what the staff were up against. I was a handful just over a week ago and I had my own example as well as others to take into consideration. Even if it wasn't my fault, even if none of it was my fault, it wasn't really their fault either.

Natural human instinct is to want answers though and sometimes to try and assign some blame helps a bit too. Let's be honest here!

I told her I had been taking notes since my stay began, trying to piece together what was happening in this nightmarish place.

She looked concerned and a little flustered too.

I said that so many things had happened and that I was shocked at the way this ward was set up.

I told her that I had taken note of many things which were wrong and many things which surprised me beyond belief.

I said I didn't want to cause any problems or get anyone in trouble and that I knew everyone was making the best of a bad situation (or something to this effect).

Once again if anyone was recording this whole process please let me have a copy, I am regurgitating this from memory, feelings, trapped emotions and lists of Miss Marple style notes.

She looked really upset and confirmed they were doing their best. I knew this.

I asked why there were no therapies or support. Nothing to help us heal. Nothing to help us let the demons out and start to rebuild our lives.

She noticed my yoga mat

I said my friend brought it for me to help me heal myself. I told her about one of the staff questioning if it was safe for me to have as it was flammable, once again I mentioned the issue being the lighters not the mat. I expressed how sad I felt about starting smoking again and that I could not believe that smoking was happening in the 'Zen garden' but I didn't want to get started on that again!

She knew what I was implying and said they used to have yoga classes but there was no funding. They simply didn't have the money to offer anything like this.

She said she knew it wasn't a good situation to be in. You don't say!

Once again I was conscious I didn't want to pile this all on her as she looked like she was already overloaded with having to cope with such a role.

She also mentioned that staff were off due to stress and breakdowns of their own.

We chatted and she told me about some of her own personal stresses and how difficult her job and also her life is working here.

I could feel her upset too. She was a lovely lady in a very stressful pressured job. She filled up with tears at one point so I decided to leave it there and said I would be speaking with my advocate and making sure things changed.

I knew I needed to write about my journey, as you have now read I had experienced far too much to keep all of this inside of me.

I also wanted to make sure I didn't put myself in another situation which would affect my sleep or my own mind which was now hopefully going to get the chance to heal from this huge ordeal.

How sad that the one place which could help people to heal actually makes it worse!

Using the broken leg analogy again, which they all seemed to love to quote so much! It had been like arriving in casualty with a broken leg and being told they were going to train me for a marathon.

I felt knackered by it all.

I told her it was my chap's birthday the following day and that I would be making him a card.

I may have told her a little bit more about myself at this point too as I was feeling excited to have the opportunity to speak with someone.

The other nurses seemed extra supportive that day too. After morning medication I didn't need any more tablets, I remember asking if I could get weighed as I wondered if all these sandwiches had laid heavy on my tummy. I got weighed in my dressing gown and felt happy I was the same.

The smiley slimming world nurse was happy too as it meant my pre-freedom weigh-in was already done. She asked me how I felt about leaving, I said nervous but excited!

The other lovely nurse made sure I got some paper to wrap the birthday present and also crafts to make the card.

I spent some time sat in the main area and had a few small chats with some of the other service users being careful not to seem too smiley or happy or celebrate my soon to be freedom. I was conscious I didn't want to tip anyone over the edge.

There was a gentle lady who had also been fronted up to by the stocky man the week before, she asked about my tea and their messages. Over the last few days I had started to leave the inspirational messages dotted around the ward for the right people to be led to at the right (or maybe wrong) time.

I told her it was Relax Tea and the messages helped me. She said she liked chamomile tea, they had chamomile in them so I said I would get her the box I had left over. I also asked if she liked to read, she said she loved to read but that there were only gardening books on the book shelf in the 'therapy room'. She told me which kind of books and it turns out I had just the one for her. I said I would go back to my room and get the tea and the book.

She welled up with tears and thanked me asking me if I was sure this was ok.

Of course it was ok!

Bless her!

Bless us all!

Today I would share little snippets of love wherever I went still conscious of not giving too much just yet but I would sprinkle some of my Liz magic on this place if that was the last thing I did before I left!

When I gave her the book and tea she cried. I saw her later on and she said it was the perfect book. I had told her I was going home and she said she was happy for me, I said to be strong and trust the process and that she could do it too.

During the last day on the ward I had more encounters with people than I had for the previous nine days.

I had a brief chat with the tattooed guy who looked after the pens in the 'Therapy room'. He was nice enough, I told him about my tattoo and my trip to Peru, I asked if he was into alternative stuff. He'd done some native American sweat lodges and seemed surprised when I said I had too. I said I was going to make my

THE DAY I GOT SECTIONED

chap a birthday card once again feeling like I didn't want to say too much or share too much of myself in that place.

The lovely Chinese lady, 'service user', was about too, she came and sat near us so I went and got the colour therapy unicorn book and pens, I showed her the pictures I had done and gestured it would help her too, she took it and started to colour in with a big smile on her face.

The gentle guy who shook a lot was about too, he'd been celebrating the birth of the royal baby that weekend, whooping and running around the corridors, I liked him, he was nice. He kept saying I would be going home but I played it down, I asked him if he had written his poem, a few days earlier he was struggling with his anxiety and suicide attempts so I suggested writing, he said he would write a poem to his wife and he was still working on it, bless him!

I decided to get ready, one last shower in the wet room. I wondered if I could find a hairdryer anywhere as I had heard one a few days before.

I didn't know if stuff like this would be allowed on the ward. The young girl who had tried to set her hair on fire the previous week was near my room, her hair looked beautiful, I asked her and she said she had a hairdryer and I could use it. One of the nurses had brought it to the ward and had it PAT tested.

BTW this was another one of the reasons I couldn't have my

charger whilst in there but on the second to last night one of the agency night staff gave me it back and said I may as well keep it. I remember feeling that paranoid about having the charger I popped in the nearest toilet and stuffed it down my jeans so as not to get caught!

Ridiculous but true. That's how I felt in there.

I had a hairdryer! Yay!

I cried as I took the last shower, letting the tears wash over me as I pressed the big red button for the hot water looking back over the past few weeks and all the hot waters I had got myself into.

I washed myself off and popped my birthstone crystal in my Yoni (yes, why not?). I felt the healing powers of the crystal and the strength in my inner core, my womb wisdom, my inner knowing that I would be ok eventually and that I could heal all of this in my own unique way.

It felt so good to dry my hair properly. I decided I would do my hair and make-up in my underwear as this felt freeing too. I'd spent so much time covering myself up, I was in my room and as far as I knew I wasn't under observation now anyway.

I felt someone looking through my window. It was one of the male staff I didn't feel comfortable with, the night before he had asked me what music I was listening to which was Oasis at the time, getting back into the music me and my chap enjoy together.

He asked me if I wanted to shoot some pool, it felt like a strange question, I told him I didn't. I'd never felt good about this guy, he was the good cop, bad cop one!

He was at my window again! I fronted up to the door and said I was drying my hair in a go away now kind of tone, he went.

I did my make-up. No more tears today my make-up was on now and I was going home. I did feel worried about the return home but at least I was getting out of this place!

Someone also dropped off a very official letter in a brown envelope for me that morning too, it said:

Elizabeth Green
Private and Confidential

My heart missed a beat as I wasn't sure what it was, to my relief it was the official letter to say my section had been lifted. PHEW!

Chapter 23

The Last Afternoon

I was like Peter Kay at this point but not in a humorous way. You know that sketch he did where he talks about the last day of your holiday when you have one last everything.

Last time in the pool.

Last ice cream.

Last view of the beach.

I was doing my own version of that in a reverse way, no sadness about leaving this place but still carrying all kinds of emotions.

Last sandwich from the fridge.

Last eye-roll when asking for said sandwich out of the fridge.

Last poo in those awful toilets with the see through door window.

Last time in the canteen.

Last fag in the Zen smoking garden.

Last time I would see this mishmash of folk.

I was feeling quite overwhelmed that afternoon but the card making took my mind off it and felt like one of the most therapeutic things I'd done all week!

That was apart from the conversations in the room where I was doing my childlike arts and crafts.

The ladies in there were lovely. I totally get that I didn't make any effort to spend time with people but as you have read on the pages before, I felt so alone and confused about everything, I was scared. I didn't know what I could or couldn't do or what support was on offer.

Not that this redefined my stay in anyway but had I known there was glue, cardboard, sequins and glitter I may have been in this room more often, I think it was open on afternoons but once again no-one told me about this and during the first week the whiteboard was a load of old bollocks to put it bluntly. Anyway been there and said that already, not meaning to sound like a stuck record here but it really does frustrate me!

Simple changes could have made all the difference.

Simple changes going forward could make a huge difference in other people's lives too!

Right, I'll get off my bandwagon again.

I had a pot of glue, four blank cards and a load of sequins and buttons.

I tried to look as normal and unchildlike as possible as I started to create some cards.

I had decided to make the one for my chap's birthday as planned and also one for my mum and dad, and my friends who came to visit me.

I was off to a bad start when I knocked the glue over but the lovely ladies rushed to help me clear it up. The glue had spilled out onto the table to form a perfect heart shape that couldn't be ignored!

I said (without trying to sound too special needs) "Wow! Look the glue has made a perfect heart shape!"

I loved signs like this!

A beautiful young woman with hair down to her waist was here at this point, she loved the glue heart as well, I vaguely remembered seeing her on the ward, but hadn't seen her enough to connect with. On this day I connected with her quite a bit, she was a service user like me and one of the ladies who worked in the room was brushing her hair for her and putting it in a plait.

As I made the cards we chatted about all kinds of stuff, I spoke about what had happened during the lead up to my breakdown

THE DAY I GOT SECTIONED

and how sad and scary it was. They both shared stories about some of the sad and scary stuff which had happened on the ward.

I did have a few pangs of anxiety in that room with everything swirling around me about what I was facing but kept making my cards and chatting. Maybe the conversations weren't really helping but it was what it was.

I'd said how shocking I had found it on the ward, she said it was hard but a fulfilling job. One of the stories they shared stuck with me. A few years ago a young guy who was a service user on the ward was playing pool, until last night I didn't even know there was a pool room, glad I didn't take up good cop, bad cop's offer now though with the story that unfolded!

Apparently this young guy was playing pool and smashed the pool queue in two and then went on to stab one of the staff with it! She described all the blood in detail and how awful it was and said some of the staff ended up having to take time off for stress.

I bet they did!

I needed stress management after being in here for ten days let alone working there.

I spoke about how sometimes we can find strength when faced with adversity and used the film The Impossible as my example. How we can bounce back from tragedy and choose to feel differently.

I said lots whilst I made those cards and could feel my Liz~ness coming back to me.

The girl with the long hair was so clever! I loved chatting with her too. A few other service users popped in and out of the room but seemed to be unable to deal with the level of conversation and left as quickly as they arrived. The smiley Chinese lady hung around, she couldn't speak English so didn't understand all the deep stuff we were chatting about anyway, bless her!

We had a bit of a laugh too and I told them about my Peaky Blinder impressions, they agreed they were crushing on Tommy Shelby too!

Haaaahaaaa!

So it wasn't just me who wanted the impressions! I just dared to say it out loud, maybe saying it to the policeman wasn't the best idea but that was in the past now.

I spoke to the girl with the long hair again later on out in the smoking garden, I was feeling the emotions welling up about going home she picked up on this and said I would be ok, she said you can do this you will be ok.

We had such a heart warming chat, she told me that she had only just come out of her shell and started talking to people after being in the ward for just over a year.

JUST OVER A YEAR ON THAT WARD?!?

WHAT!?!

My mind, body and spirit combo struggled to deal with this. Then I remembered my neighbour who'd been in the system for thirty odd years. How long had people been here?

We chatted some more and she told me she was autistic but because they hadn't been able to prove that for some time she had to stay there.

I felt appalled!

She said she wished she could have "I am autistic" tattooed to her head and shared more about her feelings and experiences.

We had a wonderful exchange of energy which I will always remember. What an amazing strong person she was!

I told her about my first book I had self- published and she said she would like to read it.

I told her a little more about me and she told me a little bit more about herself. She was leaving in about three weeks and moving into supported housing where her bunny rabbit was waiting for her. I felt so happy for her!

She also told me how bath time works. Wished I'd have know this ten days ago! She said once the 15 minute checks are over you only get checked once an hour so you could time it to be let into the bathroom and manage a 30-45 minute bath without your privacy being broken. She told me a funny story about a red bath bomb she once used without realising and had to cut her own bath short due to the colour of the water. She didn't want the emergency alarms pressing in case they thought she had tried to kill herself!

I could have sat and chatted with her for hours!

The good cop, bad cop guy came out and shouted "FOOD TIME" at us. He said "FOOD'S OUT COME GET IT NOW!!". I was less than an hour from being a free woman and really wanted to tell him where to go but instead politely said my food was in the fridge so I was in no rush.

He stormed off. She looked at me. I looked at her. She said she doesn't normally pick up on these kind of things but how wrong that felt.

I agreed, I said lots of stuff was wrong in this place.

She said she wanted to tell him to "FUCK OFF!" I said she should have and that I wanted to as well!

We smirked like kids! Then we smiled at each other and wished each other all the best.

I also had a lovely chat with my first fag supplier from the previous week.

He was sat outside with his mum

THE DAY I GOT SECTIONED

I didn't know visitors could come outside with us to the smoking garden!

She said she wasn't allowed but that she followed her own rules. A fab lady! Her son was sat with her and had a sparkle in his eye as we talked about why he was in there. He had been living in the woods, walking for miles and miles and had no fixed abode. He said he loved living in those woods so close to nature, I agreed how wonderful that would be.

She shared all about alternative therapies she was involved in back home and knew all about shamanic stuff as I explained what I was into. I wasn't sure if I liked the word shamanic anymore as I had been saying I was into shhhhh~manic practices in the months leading up to all that had happened.

Time will heal.

I loved my little chats that day and loved connecting with people a little bit more.

I also saw my second fag supplier in the canteen, she'd just been for her nose piercing. We shared tattoo stories and I took my jumper off and showed her the top piece of my back tattoo.

I could feel my new found freedom and all these little snippets of happy chats mirrored that.

It was a good job I packed in the morning as the cleaners came to strip my bed and mop up. All my stuff was piled high in one corner and a few bits and bobs remained in my safe to make sure they were safe especially all of my notes.

I'd written out my cards in my room away from all the conversations from earlier.

I wished I had asked my chap to come a little earlier but once again I trusted the process.

I went for my last fag and got a light off the guy who looked a bit like a tramp, I hadn't really spoken to him during my stay but he was a peaceful warrior and was usually the one having stuff thrown at him not the other way around. I pointed out that his rainbow lighter matched my socks and thought I'd better go get my boots on ready for the return home. I sat in the sunshine and did one last angel card reading.

I wish I could share what the angel card was with you here today, probably something really poignant but I can't really remember what my angel cards said but they did keep me going during this really difficult time.

There was a new service user on the ward, he was laid outside the main office and had covered himself in paper towels, everyone was ignoring him. I'd seen him a little earlier struggling to walk, he appeared to have really bad anxiety issues. I intended he would get more support than I had whilst on this ward.

I had text everyone to let them know I was coming home on this

THE DAY I GOT SECTIONED

day too and arranged to go to my mum and dad's to see them in a couple of days as my brother was returning home too.

My chap arrived. I was shaking like a leaf.

They told me I had to come back the following day for my official release meeting. I thought today was the last time I would ever see that place!

Gutted as we had planned to go off for the day as it was his birthday! Wishing I had made a run for it on the Tuesday when the doctor shook my hand. The nurse managed to get us the first appointment at 9am, we would have traffic to deal with but at least we still had the full day ahead of us.

My chap said he was worried I was getting institutionalised. I made a few trips to get all my bags.

I'd managed to accrue quite a lot of stuff during my stay, he said the car wasn't far. They needed to let us out. Another lady was leaving too and had all of her stuff in bin bags. This felt so surreal. I felt a whoosh of energy because I was free but yet overwhelmed by all kinds of emotions at how I would cope back in the 'real world'. I wasn't even sure what my real world would consist of anymore.

We got to the car, parking had been quite costly during my stay as well as all the stuff he had to buy me to eat. Old money worries surfaced but I did my best not to think about that. We had some good stuff to look forward to these coming weeks.

His birthday. My massage. Various breakfasts out with friends. Family time. Our mini break which I had vowed I would get booked ASAP. I hoped I'd be ok and tried not to over think.

The drive home felt odd, I kept breathing deeply. We passed the shop, I asked if we could call for a bottle of wine and told him I wasn't taking those pills anymore. I needed something to help me chill. Maybe not the best option but hey when needs must!

Chapter 24

Home Sweet Home

I didn't want to see anyone else that evening.

I went straight into the house and let him bring all the bags in. MILO! MY MILO!

Hugs and tears.

Now to see Levi and Lloyd my cats, I had missed their fur, their smell, their love and cuddles. They were there to greet me. I had missed them so much!

MY VIEW!

The fields!

The Alpacas!

My garden!

My lounge, my kitchen, my cottage!

I made my way upstairs and walked around, that familiar smell with a hint of cleaning products in the background as my chap had cleaned the house within an inch of it's life and prepared for my return home.

I went up to the attic room, my sacred space.

When I came back down hugs of all kinds were waiting for me. I popped my wine in the fridge grateful that I had some way of relaxing that evening, letting go of any wrongness I felt about drinking it, I'd had a massive detox, it'd be ok.

Apart from no wine there was one other thing that I hadn't done for over ten days, I asked my chap to guess what it was.

Can you guess?

Usually we do it every day many times.

Unless you live in a bungalow or a mental ward.

Stairs!

I was walking up and down the stairs again, my legs felt a little wobbly, our cottage has four floors with open wooden steps. I was looking forward to getting out walking again.

That night is a bit of a blur, not because of the wine but because I didn't feel like myself. We lit our real fire and watched TV, nothing out of the ordinary.

In between reintegrating myself back into my life as it was I cried lots and hugged lots.

We did watch BGT which was recorded and waiting for my return. My chap laughed and asked me if I wanted to rewatch the one from the Saturday night, I said we'd best not.

I had to take some really deep breaths while watching it and forced a few laughs too. My BGT watching days have got easier now and the Final's have been on and no-one was hurt! Yay!

We planned to get up nice and early the following morning to make sure we were on time for the 'goodbye for good' appointment.

My chap also had his 'special' card to open and his pre-chosen gift to unwrap, I was gutted I didn't get chance to get him any birthday surprises but he was happy to have me home so nothing like this mattered much anyway.

Traffic was bad so I called ahead to say we would be about 15 minutes late which was ok.

The doctor passed me in the corridor and said hello, I felt like a little girl. I felt annoyed too. We went through the security doors to go back in and into the smallest of the visiting rooms.

I wasn't sure where I could or couldn't go at this point I was between two worlds, home and the ward.

It was the lovely slimming world nurse who checked me out with a few short questions she apologised for asking and a bag with five tablets in, one per day for the next five days to help with my integration back to life I assumed.

She asked:

"Are you likely to try and harm yourself?"

Nope.

"Are you likely to try and harm anyone else?"

I laughed a little and said I was more likely to try and hug everyone I saw rather than harm them. She laughed too.

Now for a wild synchronicity!

Outside our visiting room was a familiar face. It was a lady who attends the same yoga class as me and has for years. Bearing in mind there are only eight of us in yoga and the ward was well outside the area where we both lived.

I did a double take.

At this point I had my wellies and bright blue raincoat on with my favourite bright yellow hat with red and blue feathers on the top. I had checked in with my chap that morning to make sure I didn't look too 'crazy' in said outfit and hat but I did feel a little bold at this point.

I just looked like Liz to her. Liz in a mental hospital, what was going on?

She said "Ohhhh helloooo, what are you doing here?"

I didn't know what to say so asked the same question back. It turned out she is a social worker.

I told her I had been sectioned here and was just checking out. We both did the wide-eyed, I don't know what to say right now emoji face and she smiled saying what a small world it was.

I said we must talk, we must go for coffee at some point.

How very synchronistic.

I felt like the Universe and the angels were saying it's ok Liz, you are completely supported here.

I'm now back at yoga class, I felt a mix of nerves and excitement to see her and fill in that piece of the jigsaw as well as seeing everyone and getting back to that 'normal' part of my life. We had a good chat and it became clear that everything unfolded as it did due to it being a Sunday, no-one was available to support my situation. No protocol was followed. So sad.

After this 'chance meeting' we left the ward and went back to the car.

That was it - Job done.

Well that part of the journey was over, now came the daunting bit, getting back to Liz Land which is still an ongoing journey. Writing is helping so thank you for being here.

Our day in Hope Valley was magical. I had taken one of the tablets first thing that morning to help calm the underlying anxiety.

Normally a trip to such a beautiful place wouldn't cause me any negative feelings, far from it but things were different that day.

The drive was beautiful, door to door countryside and little lambs everywhere. On the way there we had another magical moment, I made sure it was real and not imagined as I pointed out some tiny lambs in a field wearing little orange rain jackets, they even had hoods! Harking back to the weekend I was losing it when we first saw lambs wearing rain coats. We pulled over and took a photo to check they were real, as we laughed and giggled at how cute they looked.

The views and the lambs were my main focus that day. We've done this walk a number of times before and midweek you don't come across many other people there. It was particularly quiet that day as we chatted, held hands, admired the view and gave thanks for living so near to such wonderful places.

Thank goodness for nature nurture!

We walked slowly and stopped often, I was still feeling a bit floaty as this was the first time I'd walked anywhere other than corridors, tea runs and to and from the smoking garden. My wellies felt sooooo good! Like an old pair of comfy slippers, I loved holding Milo's lead too!

We adopted Milo five years ago, he's had some issues with anxiety and aggression and sometimes doesn't know how to react to situations. He has to stay on his lead and is sometimes a handful. I recalled how well behaved he was at the hospital the weekend before when he visited. He felt a lot calmer this day and even sat down near the lambs and gave a paw. He knew it was healing time.

We sat by a beautiful stream, had a smoke and celebrated freedom and birthdays, I felt ok but wondered if this was the initial feelings of elation and the pill I had taken.

There's a lovely church at the end of the walk. I love to go in old churches, as you know I'm not religious but I like to see the old buildings and the stained glass windows.

I also like to have a nosy at the book shelves they often have in churches to see if any interesting books pop out. I was a little freaked out when I saw a copy of the Salem Witch Trials!

I read the cover and flicked through the pages wondering if I should make a donation and take it home, I didn't have any cash on me so mentioned it to my chap when I'd found him outside looking at the old gravestones, he said he didn't think that was the right kind of book to be reading right now after all I had been through, I agreed.

Strange 'sign' though nonetheless!

We went to our favourite little heritage cafe where all the profits go back into the local area and beautiful walks. I felt happy and smiled at the lovely ladies behind the counter, there were knitted robins everywhere too, I said they were cute and we had a nice chat about robins.

I ordered two lattes and a cream scone for each of us and they didn't even charge me extra for the syrup. I felt tearful because they had been so nice to me, I hoped this would wear off as I couldn't start welling up every time I encountered a nice person, it was all fresh and new so I forgave myself and thanked them for being so nice!

I forgot to ask for the coffees in a take out cup as we were sat outside, my chap wasn't happy, it was no big deal but he wanted a take out cup to keep his coffee warm. In the early stages of my release little things like this really tipped me over the edge as I felt useless and wrong, like I couldn't even do simple things in life anymore.

The scones were lovely, so was the coffee.

I asked if we could call at another one of the local villages on the way home so I could buy myself some new earrings to mark my release, I also wanted to look for some surprise birthday gifts. I knew which shop I would go to, every time we've been in before the ladies have been so lovely and helpful.

They nearly made me cry too. I said I had just got out of hospital, they were polite enough not to ask what I had been in for, not sure what I would have said if they did, I hadn't thought that far ahead. They were extra kind! I chose some earrings and even though I knew I hardly had any money in my account I let go of any money worries and looked at the crystals they were selling too hoping there would be a skull I could get my chap. No crystal eggs today, I had enough of those at home! My latest batch of stock had been delivered whilst I was in hospital but I couldn't even begin to think about continuing to set up my business, I hoped the excitement would return again soon.

The only crystal skull they had looked to have a funny face so I decided to pick a strange looking penguin which looked like two people hugging from different angles. It reminded me of the Penguin book my mum had, be dignified yet flippant. Ok.

Then, just before I paid I spotted a very exciting display near the counter.

IT WAS A WHOLE DISPLAY OF WISH STRINGS!

OMG!!

My chap had exhausted the stock at our local post office. I was giddy! I told the lady in the shop how he'd brought me these every day to the hospital and showed her my wrists. I wondered if there was a more masculine one I could get him and there was!

It was more than perfect! An infinity sign on a black string, saying to infinity and beyond!

I bought it and eyed up a mermaid one I liked. I knew when this particular gift was opened that my chap would be taking lots of motorbike rides here and there would be many more Wish Strings to come.

Once again I felt the Universe and the angels were speaking to me through synchronicity saying it's ok Liz, you are totally supported.

As I type this here today I feel relief to be writing about my first days of freedom, I have my iPod on shuffle, I listen to more music these days and have also found it helps me to type faster too, who knew!

The shuffle is playing the perfect songs. James Blunt (I know sorry! heehee), the song, One Of The Brightest Stars has just come on, saying one day your story will be told. Yes it will!

We called at the shop on the way home and I picked up a fancy bottle of wine. I decided to drink less wine but choose a better quality bottle even though I didn't really have the cash to spend. I let go of that worry, we would get there, it'd all be ok.

We had a lovely evening cuddled on the sofa with the fire on and watched some films and ate nice food. I was really happy to be home again.

It was time to take each day as it comes and be in the moment. I knew we were going to mum and dad's the next day and I would see my brother too. It's been a number of years since I had seen him as he has been living abroad. I would have felt a little nervous under normal circumstances, after all I'd gone through, things felt blown out of any normal proportion. I flashed back to a few weeks before this when I thought he'd been in an attack. He was alive! Everyone was! It was all ok!

I had some nightmares and woke myself up panicking a few times during the night, that posh wine obviously hadn't worked its wonders.

At least I had hugs and support now.

I was switching my phone off a lot during the first few weeks. I didn't feel able to cope with any kind of information overload. My yoga friend had sent me a message the night before to see if I wanted to go to our local ice cream parlour and cafe for breakfast, I knew it would be busy but I said yes and took another one of those tablets to calm my nerves.

It helped me feel more relaxed, I washed my hair and put my make-up on, no tears today.

We had a lovely breakfast, it was busy but we were too busy chatting for me to notice. I shared stories from the ward and thanked my friend again for all of her support. We laughed at the funny stuff I shared and I felt ok.

I got home and felt good, I was back, I could do this!

She had also given me a lovely welcome home gift with a candle to light the darkest of times, a little note pad to write both my negative and positive feelings to share with friends and get support and a posh bubble bath. How nice!

I had her card and yoga stuff but dropped it off later that day. It was a simple card covered in circular sequins in as many colours as possible, I'd kept it light inside, put a message of gratitude and finished it off with love from your 'special' friend.

Next on the agenda was to go back to mum and dad's, the home in which I had grown up from a teenager into an adult. The home in which just less than two weeks earlier I lost my mind and did some crazy stuff I was still deeply judging myself for.

What did the neighbours think?

How much of a fool had I made of myself?

I hoped I would cope with going back to the scene of the crime, all those police people! The ambulance, the noise, the dragging me out of the house, the bit where my dad fell on me on the stairs!

The stuff I said! This was a BIG DEAL.

My family are amazing, to them there was no big deal, they kept it nice and relaxed.

On the drive over there I had flashbacks.

It felt as if I could go back in time and put myself back in that place again.

Keep it together Liz. Stay grounded.

We had fish on Friday and a glass of wine, the tablet had worn off by then and I needed it to calm my shattered nerves.

It was really surreal to see my brother. I couldn't hug him properly as he'd been in an accident the night before, fallen down the stairs, cut his head open and knocked himself out as well as bruising all of his ribs.

I had a flashback to the bit where I was shouting at my dad telling him to come downstairs as I thought he was going to fall down the stairs on that dreaded Sunday. Was this connected? Strange goings on!

We had a little hug and I did my best to be as normal as possible, I wasn't sure what normal was but I did my best not to come out with anything too silly. We are a family who likes to laugh and can often be found using the laughter is the best medicine life principle so we did have a chuckle at some of the things we reminisced about, I think it was too soon for my dad to laugh though, he stayed in the kitchen cooking.

We returned home.

I was struggling to have the courage to wander up the lane with Milo on his evening walk, I didn't want to go on my own, sometimes I didn't even feel like going at all which wasn't like me.

That weekend we also visited our best friends who live a few doors away, I had flashbacks to a few weeks earlier when I was running up and down the street trying to keep everyone safe.

It was lovely to see them and I delivered my hand made 'Special' card which was covered in buttons as one of them has a button phobia which we've always joked about. This is also where the Tommy wants a snickers joke came from, something from years ago, I had bought them a pack of those dreadful Snickers chocolate bars as well, they said looser, messed up, knackered and something else equally as awful on them. I also laughed a little and asked for a high five, awkward but heart felt laugh time and a few sideways glances we saw the humour.

Laughter's the best medicine!

I love that we all have such similar and sometimes wrong senses of humour.

My best friend took me out for another breakfast too, this time up to the farm shop where I thought my chap was being attacked exactly two weeks ago, it wasn't as busy and there was no horsing event on that day but I still got flashbacks on the way there. I'd taken a tablet so that helped me stay calm.

We went on lots of walks that weekend too, choosing the quiet ones to help healing.

I was open and honest with people in the village when they asked why they hadn't seen me in a while and told my neighbours what had happened. Hugs and tears all round, I felt so grateful to live in such a wonderful and supportive community.

My chap's sister and husband came to visit this weekend too and we went for a walk and some ice cream, I relayed everything which had happened even though it made me feel trippy and tired by this point but I had to get it up and out. I appreciated the listening ears and the ice cream was lovely, the sun was shining and it felt like summer was on the way.

Thank goodness I hadn't come out to the long bleak winter we'd just experienced, it has its own weather system up here in the hills! Thank you sunshine!

Chapter 25

The First Week Of Freedom

I had two of the five tablets left after the weekend and found another two which they must have given me on that first night out. I didn't want to get any more prescription drugs after these so kept them for busy or anxious days.

I planned a few big walks out on my own with Milo, once again places I knew would be quiet which I could walk to from our cottage as I didn't feel balanced enough to drive.

I did three huge walks that week around all of the local countryside and for the first time in years even had the courage to walk through the middle of a cow field. Maybe it was the tablets helping me?

On the Monday I decided to take my own bull by the horns and let everyone know why I had been missing in the online world. My spiritual friend had put a note in my private groups to say I was taking some healing time in case anyone wondered where I was, she also made a video to give a brief little share on what had happened. Bless her!

I posted the following:

'This time 2 weeks ago I woke up in a mental hospital.....

I share this from the centre of my heart as part of my healing process for all of those who know me well I speak my truth.... Its gonna take time and courage and I am still in a healing process reintegrating back into my life at home after my release I'm so grateful to have nature all around me my amazing chap whose strength n love got me through this as well as my family (ma n pa I love you!) and my close friends thank you for being here in your own unique and very special ways

This time 2 weeks ago I woke up in the most scary place I've ever been after a time of taking care of a friend with mental health issues not realizing how much I'd been out of my routine and also giving far too much of myself (I know it's one of my traits ~ but not a bad one at that ~ lesson learnt !)

After days without sleep & being in fight flight mode for days due to pressures of "trying" to hold space for someone else's healing as well as others involved in the situation I had a nervous breakdown

Something popped in my brain and life became surreal for me it was deep set fears coming up.... I genuinely feared for my safety and the safety of those around me

I've never experienced any mental health issues first hand I know I'm always the funny one and laughter helps me cope and I know in my heart that everything happens for a reason.... but I'm serious my laughter went as did my humour for a while....

I was sectioned by the mental health act in a very scary mixed ward thrown out of the frying pan into the fire

I cannot unsee what I've experienced

Some of it broke my heart

Some of it scared me

Some of it brought sadness I've never felt before

I documented everything I experienced

I know sharing this here today will help too

There'll be more to come all in good time

I want to honor everyone's own journey and can only speak from my own experiences but after I'd had a few nights sleep I started to see the truth of the situation

My door didn't lock

Sirens were going off all night

People running up and down the corridors trying to do their best to help very poorly people

I had no privacy

THE DAY I GOT SECTIONED

I felt imprisoned

I felt ashamed

I felt weak

I felt I'd lost my liz~ness

But I knew self preservation was key

Gradually I started to reconnect with me

With Liz green

Who I am

What I stand for

For now my chap my family my friends and this beautiful place in which I live and of course magical Milo my labradoodle and all of the animals around me will support my Healing

I will write about my story

I will share

When the times right

Trusting the process

Trusting myself and my truth

If you read this thank you

Only comment if you feel drawn to

I have an advocate and am organizing counseling for myself to help this process

It's time for me to deeply practice what I preach......

Rebirth

It had over 200 comments within a few days, the love and support was immense, it made me cry lots. Everyone was being so lovely, maybe it was ok, maybe I was ok. I also got lots of email messages from people who had been in similar situations but daren't speak up, they thanked me for my openness which supported their healing too. A few people also sent me articles about the experiences of shamans spending time in mental hospitals and how intense it can be when you feel so much on this level.

In the now, as I type these words, it was exactly a month ago today I posted that and now here I am, the book nearly finished! It's amazing what we can create when we put our heart and soul into it, when we have a mission, a purpose, a calling!

I guess I am doing ok. I think.

Walking gave me lots of time to heal, when I was on my own I would connect with the magic of the outdoors, when I walked with my chap I would talk about what happened and cry sometimes. I was certain he was sick of hearing about the ward, I was like the Band Camp Girl in the American Pie films. "This one time at the mental hospital!!"

Now, a little further along I'm still like her but the wording has changed.

"This one time in my book!!"

Bless my chap!

Bless me

I spoke to friends on the phone and texted people too to say I was out and on my healing journey at home which in fairness was the start of my healing process, shame there was no healing in that bloody hospital just the making worse of things!

Gone but not forgotten.

We had arranged to see my chap's mum and dad too. It was so lovely to see them, lots to share and open up about, I was so grateful for their unconditional love and support too.

It felt good to be opening up and sharing the truths of what had unfolded.

I would keep going.

Keep being honest about my feelings.

Keep opening up.

I had a message from a medical person this week too. There was no number but I googled where they were calling from, the name of the place sounded like a retreat. Maybe it was time to have that retreat I had wished, hoped and dreamed for whilst on the ward.

Nope.

It turns out it was a lovely nurse from the NHS doing his follow up. We chatted on the phone, he said I sounded like a confident woman and he was looking forward to meeting me. I said we were hoping to book a few nights away in the Lakes and the Dales the following week which our friend had gifted us so arranged to see him the week after, he said he would come to my house which was nice. I assumed this was to make sure I wasn't in a crazy state and was taking care of myself. I arranged for my chap to be free for the meeting too in case Milo was barking so we could be nice and relaxed and calm.

I spent quite a bit of time that week calling around trying to find somewhere to stay the following week. Before the week was up I manifested the perfect dog friendly place to stay which was in between the Lakes and the Dales, the perfect place to visit all our fave places.

Yesssssss!

The lady I booked with was amazing. I told her I was fresh out of hospital, once again she didn't ask why which made it easy but she did say the room would be the perfect retreat as it had a lovely big bathroom and bath too.

THE DAY I GOT SECTIONED

WHOOHOOOO!

I danced round the kitchen, phoned my chap and text my best friend to say a HUGE THANK YOU for gifting us this mini break!

The first few weeks were easier than the weeks which followed, everyone rallied round and I had lots to keep me busy. I knew at some point life had to return to normal, or as normal as it could be.

I flashed back to the thoughts I had of lotto wins and felt fed-up that we didn't have much money and that due to my temporary imprisonment we had even less now.

I did my best and am still doing my best to take each day as it comes and trust this whole big massive process called life. As we all are.

I booked my Thai spa massage too.

I chose the Tuesday as me and my mum also had tickets to go and see a theatre show that evening.

I think we went for fish on Friday again at the end of that week. I also shared a few more bits on social media, mainly pictures of my views on all of our walks, it kept me company taking pictures to share.

We had a chilled weekend. Nothing out of the ordinary to report. The nightmares and emotions had started to become a regular occurrence now and I had run out of tablets.

We went to get some nice food from the shop and some more wine, I had to do my breathing exercise at the shop as it felt busy and reminded me of that sea of people in the ward making me feel sickly and off balance.

The first two weeks consisted of a little wine each evening, maybe not the best way to heal but we waited until later on, it helped me to sleep, I wasn't suppressing through alcohol, but it helped.

Chapter 26

Theatrical Madness And A Mini Break

The Thai spa massage was gorgeous! The theatre was crazy and cancelled out that afternoon's relaxed shoulders and feelings of ease.

The show was three hours long and we were front row, it was totally overwhelming.

I had spent the last two days worrying about it but didn't say anything as I wanted to be strong and get back into life.

Just before I was due to set off and drive to the city I broke down, I felt massive anxiety and couldn't do it! My chap said he would drive us, I didn't want to let my mum down either. For the past year or so we've had mother daughter Tuesdays planned in, I wasn't going to let these feelings stop me.

She told me afterwards she didn't know how I held things together as it was a very loud and in your face show but I did it with the help of a very large glass of wine in the pre-show bar!

We didn't get back until gone midnight and had planned to set off early doors on our mini break the next morning. We decided to get up a little later and take it easy.

I was learning that I had to slow things down and know that it's ok to say no if something didn't feel right.

I didn't have to meet any demands.

I didn't have to follow through on plans.

That said, our mini break was totally amazing!

There were a few blips on a personal level but it was just what the doctor ordered!

Every little thing about it was in alignment. Another arrangement sent on angels wings.

The place we were staying was more like a little apartment than a room in a pub, we had our own little annex, the only dog friendly room which meant we didn't have any worries with Milo being around other dogs. We had breakfast on our own in the bar area which was fab! Chill time!

On the way there we listened to our favourite tunes, called at the Starbucks we visited when in hospital and breathed a sigh of relief. We planned a stop in the Dales to visit the place we'd been a few months earlier for my 40th birthday. This was where

I declared my life had begun and it was a fresh start, I would re-do that declaration and make sure someone was listening this time.

Fresh start forties take two!

We called at the farm shop for take away coffee, we walked to the cove, we reminisced and held hands.

I felt happy.

I still felt uncertain about the future but put it to the back of my mind during this trip and made the most of every single moment.

I was alive!

We were alive!

Life's Good!

We had a walk through the local woods once we'd settled into our new abode, I felt uncomfortable being in a new place, the woods felt a bit too enclosed. I kept breathing deeply and did my best not to pass out due to the feelings of anxiety.

We went to the local town for takeaway food and managed to land on a really nice restaurant who did takeaways too, I was in my comfy leggings by this point and didn't feel like sitting in a restaurant, plus Milo might misbehave if any other dogs came in.

We ate our pizzas, drunk wine and watched a really naff film.

The TV had got stuck on one channel so we had no choice but to watch the next film up. Synchronistically enough it was about walking a pilgrimage. We love films like this and I was reading another one of Paulo Coelho's books specifically about the pilgrimage trail as well so it was meant to be.

The following day we had planned to go to another one of our fave places in the Lakes which has a magical little gypsy caravan on the walk where you can get traditional gypsy teas and scones with cream too!

It was lovely and sunny and warm. We listened to more of our favourite music in the car on the way there, I felt happy again.

We walked, we talked, we held hands, we smiled at the baby ducklings, we said hi to passers by and took pictures of the views. We stopped for a fag every now and again with a slight undertone of disappointment that we were still smoking. What a shame but we decided one baby step at a time, after the mini break we would detox from the alcohol.

We needed the loo so walked into the local village, it was really busy and warm which made me feel swirly and sick. I went in a shop for a bottle of water but had to come back out. I kept getting these blips.

Flashbacks, tension, anxiety, tears.

What on earth was wrong with me, the sun was shining and I

was FREE.

I told myself to get a grip and pull myself together. It was only 2pm when we got back to the car, we had only been out for about three hours, so decided to visit a new place on the way back to our accommodation.

On the way there we rescued a lamb which was stuck in a fence. I felt ok now.

The place we visited was by the sea but the tide was over some sand dunes and far away, there was a promenade along the front with a railway line running alongside it. The views were wonderful but I was feeling a little wobbly by this point. Deep breaths Liz, enjoy yourself you are on holiday nothing to worry about right now!

We called at a little cafe on the front, I ordered lattes and a panini each and we sat outside with Milo, there were hardly any people about and everyone was friendly. A train whizzed past, our food was ready, get set go! Everything seemed like it was in fast forward again and my heart started racing, I felt out of control and couldn't focus on our conversation. It was like I was in a tunnel, for no reason I felt that fight or flight moment. I didn't feel like my usual happy self anymore.

I needed to get out of there!

I told my chap how I felt, it made me need the loo and quick!

What the hell was going off?

I'd experienced slight feelings of panic before due to the nature of Meniere's disease but these feelings were much stronger. Very frenzied. A need to escape for no reason.

We walked back along the promenade trying to stay as calm as possible.

The only toilet was one of those 20p ones which gives you 15 minutes to do your business, it was like stepping in to some weird space ship toilet, not the best for how I was feeling!

There was a picture on the wall behind the silver metal toilet, it was a picture of an outside toilet hut from India saying this particular toilet was twinned with the place it pictured, very strange.

I tried to breathe as deeply as I could smelling the stale disinfected flavour air, watching the timer count down, I felt like I was going to pass out or that the toilet was going to swallow me up and I would disappear forever!

I managed to pull it together, sorted myself out and noticed the timer had only counted 4 minutes and 44 seconds, 444 an angel number sign! My angels were with me!

My chap was waiting for me outside with Milo and a worried looking face, we managed to get back to the car, maybe I had done too much?

I needed to get back to our accommodation.

The CD was playing a really sad song from Nashville about we are water and tears flowing, my tears were flowing thick and fast by this point. I tried to explain what I was feeling it was uncontrollable, like it wasn't me and there was nothing I could do about it.

My make-up was streaming down my face as I wiped away the tears with an old tissue I'd found in the door pocket, we were having such an amazing day, where had all of this come from?

After a while the feelings subsided and we even managed to call at the shop on the way back for some wine and nibbles, I couldn't face going out again.

Maybe the wine wasn't helping but we were on holiday and I needed something to help me sleep.

We watched a film that evening and went to sleep early.

The next morning I didn't feel 100% again at breakfast, I didn't feel much like eating and wanted to get back to the room. I kept it together as we packed our stuff away and checked out.

We visited a beautiful woods on the way home where I'd spent lots of my weekends on retreat doing shamanic practices, it's peaceful and magical.

I still felt uneasy but chatted my way through it and breathed in the fresh air from the trees in between a few roll-ups!

There was a nature retreat happening and people were randomly dotted about laid in the grass, I smiled as I remembered all of the magic I had experienced here in the past, I didn't feel like that stuff was for me anymore though, not at the moment, plus I didn't feel anywhere near confident enough to be booking myself on some retreat and meeting loads of new people.

It was then I realised this shit was going to take some time to heal. I am a person who likes things to happen quickly and I always used to have a plan, it seemed now more than ever I was going to have to go with the flow and take each day as it comes.

We called at Starbucks on the way home, the taste of the sweet caramel frappuccino and the cream on top made me feel a little better.

I was worried about the weeks ahead.

The stuff I used to do.

The stuff I didn't feel like doing anymore.

How was I going to fit back into this thing called life and create a living?

I always used to feel so inspired, yes like everyone I had my off days but I would always pick myself up, dust myself off and crack on. I was an inspired action taker most of the time but I no longer felt the inspiration.

I knew I wanted to write as this has always been a huge passion for me but I knew it was too soon, plus people were telling me to take it easy, to give myself time.

We called at my mum and dad's on the way back for some food, this way we didn't have to worry about shopping or cooking.

It was nice to see them and we had lots of stuff to talk about sharing what we'd been up to. I told them about my 'blips' and they said that was natural and not to worry.

We met up with some more of our friends at the weekend, talked some more and re-told my story of what had happened. I felt shaky most of the time and appreciated warm hugs from friends. I did my best not to breakdown whilst I relayed what had unfolded and saved the tears for when I got home again or when my chap went back to work and I was alone again.

I replied to messages, returned calls and did my best to be as normal as possible. Sometimes I felt I was talking about it too much and was conscious I needed to ask my friends how they were doing and what they had been up to. I found it hard to focus and listen to conversations, I still felt consumed by what had happened.

I just wanted to feel better again.

How long was thing going to take?

Life felt surreal.

I felt surreal.

Chapter 27

Back Home Again

The following week I had the follow up booked on the Wednesday and a meeting with the advocate on the Friday. My chap said he would support me with both of the meetings, I felt nervous and didn't know what to expect.

That weekend we did our best to settle back into our usual routine with walks, nice food, films, TV and of course some more wine. I set the intention to stop with the mid-week drinking and have a detox after that weekend.

In our infinite wisdom we decided to start watching '13 Reasons Why' again on Netflix, the second season was due out the following Friday so we wanted to refresh our memories and knew it was a really gripping show which would keep us occupied on an evening.

Maybe not the best programme to be watching when your brain is healing from a breakdown but I am a big believer in healing through emotions which are triggered by such things.

I'm not talking about soap operas and the like, for me I prefer to watch things with deeper meanings. This programme certainly covered that off!

It's about teenage bullying and suicide and has some really graphic scenes, there are helpline numbers at the beginning and the end, some of the issues covered reminded me of what I had been through.

That week I struggled to sleep.

I was determined to cut out alcohol, which I did.

I didn't want to take any prescribed medications for what I was feeling as they numbed me and made me feel like I was drinking wine anyway, I didn't want to feel like this all the time. I wanted my inspiration back, I wanted to connect with life again and feel the magic!

I was really conscious that I needed to make sure I was sleeping enough so spent a lot of that week taking naps during the day in between floating around the house and trying to be as normal as I could.

I didn't feel like doing anything.

I had the mother of all headaches which lasted nearly the whole week, I never used to get headaches, it was unbearable!

I had to take headache tablets to try and ease it, I got some herbal Kalms tablets and some Rescue Remedy too.

This week was really hard. I was ebbing and flowing between needing to do something productive and then not feeling I wanted to do anything at all other than feel sorry for myself and sleep.

I did share a few little posts online about how I was feeling and did my best to be as honest as possible, this helped too when people sent me lovely comments back. I also spoke with a few friends on the phone but I couldn't pull myself up again, it was hard to just snap out of it as it felt so deep.

I was listening to songs on the iPod that carried memories and kept dipping in and out of what had happened.

We followed the first season of '13 Reasons Why' with the second one which was really thought provoking but also filled with some ridiculous synchronicities from my own personal experiences about how life can affect your mental health.

On a side note, we were also watching the first series of 'The Handmaid's Tale' which is filled with synchronicities from what I thought was happening during my psychosis. Men taking over the world and making women swap partners and do things they don't want to all in the name of religion. Strange stuff!

The guy who came on the Wednesday was a nurse, he was gentle and kind and made me feel at ease.

I asked him what his follow up was for and he said he was just checking in and that I could share as much or as little as I wanted.

We talked all about what had happened and went over the gory details again. He was shocked, he'd never worked directly on that ward but said it must have been hard.

He even said I should write a book about my experience and joked that he would see me sharing my story on This Morning TV.

I laughed and told him that's exactly what I was going to do, write about my story with the intention of healing along the way. He said it would be so useful, even for the staff and nurses to read about mental health from the patient's perspective as he explained it's easy to become desensitised when you are in that kind of environment all of the time.

I felt empathy for all of those people on the ward doing the best they could but I knew I had to start writing soon otherwise I may be consumed by my own thoughts of it all.

He signed me off and said I was doing great and had an amazing support system to help me through this. We joked about the name badges and my need to check them all when I got sectioned, we hadn't seen his badge at this point and joked that he may have knocked on the wrong door then two hours later he's got bleeding ears after hearing the tales of my woe.

He was great! When he was leaving I showed him my garden

and the 'imaginary' alpacas I'd missed so much, he thought it was magical too.

My chap had to get back to work so they both left and I was back on my own again.

I've always enjoyed my own space but it didn't feel the same anymore, thoughts racing around my head, flashbacks, emotions bubbling up. I decided to go back to bed and sleep it off.

My chap was surprised when he came home and I burst into tears, he thought I seemed fine but dredging all of that shit up again left me feeling really vulnerable wondering if I would ever get through it all.

Plus my head was killing me!

I tossed and turned most nights and when I did sleep the dreams were nasty. I considered getting up during the night but didn't want to over stimulate myself or my tender brain. During this week I had thoughts about death again and how hard life was.

I wondered if ending things would be easier.

I'd snap out of it pretty quickly and knew I had to write this book and get myself back on track.

Tensions were building up towards the end of the week as the meeting with the advocate drew nearer. She was a truly lovely lady who was simply there to help me get my voice heard about everything which had happened so it was a good thing but anything out of the ordinary and even the day to day ordinary stuff was putting me on edge at this point.

I no longer felt that comfortable doing my beautiful morning walks with Milo let alone a trip to another city to talk about everything again.

She text the evening before to see if we could change plans and meet at a coffee shop in the centre of a different but still nearby city. I said yes with a big gulp and told my chap I was glad he was coming with me as there was no way I could do this all on my own.

I thought about all of the people who do go through this kind of stress alone and how hard it must be!

The meeting with the advocate went really well, I felt that confidence I had on the ward when I had to look out for myself again. I even cracked a few jokes and had a bit of a giggle about some of the stuff which had happened.

She took lots of notes and advised me about what action I could take. We could write to the hospital with my complaints and findings and ask for an apology or for changes to be made.

I still don't know how I feel about this, maybe I should send them a copy of this book as a letter might not be long enough to get all of my points across?

I didn't feel an apology would do much good at this point but I wanted to do my best to make a difference in the world, that's why I am sharing this, as well as part of my own healing process maybe it can help others too?

I told her about my plans for this book, she spoke about her past and said she would love to write a book too, I said I could help her and that we could support each other, which we are.

At some point we have another meeting planned in and I've invited her to my little cottage where we can hopefully sit in the sunshine in the garden and have a nice cuppa tea too. Let's see what unfolds.

I was relieved it was Friday and I could have a glass of wine after my mid week abstinence. To be honest the wine that weekend made me more emotional and as we continued watching the suicide programme I was having more nightmares connected with my own life and death feelings. Please don't judge me about the wine but it helped me to cope, as I'm sure it does for many people.

The following day it was lovely and sunny, it was Saturday but I didn't feel much like doing anything weekendy so decided the best action step I could take was to start my book, this book. So I did.

That was just under two weeks ago, 300 pages later and a lot of delving here I am.

We had a pizza on the Saturday night and watched a film. Sunday we had traditional chicken dinner even though it was warm. The little things were the things which kept me going and of course my writing too, which as you have experienced here first hand is far from anything little.

Chapter 28

And So It Is.....

I spent the next few weeks writing every day, I was so grateful the sun kept shining. The headaches were few and far between and I'd even started to laugh about some of the goings on as I typed them here for you to read.

It's been the biggest most surreal journey of my life including recounting everything that happened.

I figure if I can do this in such a short space of time anything is possible, plus if I really was 'damaged' in some way how would I be able to write all of this?

I do feel quite proud of myself for getting through this but I know that's going to take time as well. The excitement pops back in to say hi every now and again and I do feel hope for the future but I am not sure what it holds anymore.

In between my writing I have shared a couple of videos in my private groups online with updates and some Emotional Freedom Technique tapping to help clear the contrast that's arising.

I am booked in for some counselling with a local voluntary group and have been given the details for some Cognitive Behavioral Therapy via the doctors.

Another little funny story. When I called to make the appointment I asked to see a female doctor as this felt more comfortable to me, plus I didn't want to end up seeing the doctor I'd seen before the whole sectioning event. The receptionist told me it would be about three weeks until I could see someone, good job I feel stronger hey! She asked me what it was with regards to and when I told her she said I could get in sooner with the doctor who is the specialist in mental health care, guess who that was! DR DEATH!

I don't think so do you!

I visited the doctors and was shocked to see some of my notes. I am going through the process of requesting copies of all my medical notes which isn't an easy task. The notes confirmed I was completely misunderstood. It brought up feelings of sadness as well as frustration and some anger. I haven't always dealt with anger very well but I am allowing the feelings to surface and trusting my counselling sessions will help me to heal these feelings.

I'll bide my time and hope that the precious thing we call time does heal the internal wounds I have suffered. The actual bruises have gone now but the bruises inside still remain. This has helped though. Sharing this with all of you. Thank you once again for being here, taking part in my story.

It's been the hardest experience of my life, the more I share what happened the more I realise how messed up it all was. I am still struggling to get back to 'normal' life, I have to take each day as it comes.

When I feel the need to cry, I cry.

When I feel the need to wax lyrical about what happened I allow myself the space to do that.

My heart was broken in two, my whole world shifted and it's taking time to process. Some days are good some not so good. I still have some sleepless nights or wake up in the early hours with uncontrollable thoughts rushing around my mind, going over what happened.

I have experienced thoughts of suicide, I won't do it, I wouldn't do it, I have too much to live for but those thoughts have still arisen. Thank goodness for all of the love and support I have around me. We need to make sure others have this support too and save peoples' lives!

I find it hard to have courage to go anywhere too busy or make too many plans. When we have something planned in it takes me to a place of anxiety in case I can't cope. I am coping though. I am doing my best to live this thing called life.

Sometimes deep feelings of loss arise and I wonder if I can carry on or how things will unfold. Life still feels hard in many ways, the things I had planned to do are on the back burner. I don't plan as much and pray to the angels to support me each day, to show me the next best steps to take.

I have started to learn to love, or at least like myself again, to worry less and trust the process more and more. To put into practice all of the things I have been teaching over the years and rebuild my life.

It's hard. Really hard.

Thank goodness I am surrounded by the beauty of nature and such amazing people. Without this support I'm really not sure I would be here now. That's what sticks with me, what about those people who don't have anyone?

People who don't have support?

The ones who are stuck in the system and can't find a way out. Or the ones who do find a way out but can't cope on the outside world.

What happens to them?

Something MUST change!

I have all kinds of feelings bubbling up now this process of the book is coming to an end, can I do this?

Will I get this out into the world?

What if I don't, how will I cope?

Is it safe for me to share this story?

What will happen to me?

Will I get into trouble?

Will I get sectioned again?

Will I offend people?

Will people think I am actually crazy after all?

Then a little voice inside says "What have you got to lose Liz, you thought you'd lost everything anyway!"

It's time for me to rebuild my life and put myself back together one step at a time.

Every now and again I connect with a new strength I have never experienced before. I have learned to trust myself on a much deeper level and listen to my inner guidance more. I am starting to learn to trust myself again and forgive myself for what happened.

I can feel a glimmer of the peace returning.

I send that love and that peace to all of you too and everyone who crossed my path during this time. Letting go of any grudges and frustration as much as I can. Tuning back into what I believe and living it.

It's not about what we are experiencing in our lives it's how we feel about it.

We can take inspired action and change our lives seeing the challenges we face as opportunities for change. That's just what I will do and I pray good things come from this.

Please forgive me.

I'm sorry.

Thank you.

I love you.

Afterword

I fulfilled my intention and finished the first draft of this book in two weeks. I know this is just the beginning and I am going to trust the process. I've had a counselling assessment, starting to go through stuff with another person from the beginning again was really hard. I now have my first full counselling session booked in and will see where this takes me.

As I mentioned earlier, I went to see the doctor and got a glimpse of my medical notes, it turns out I was seriously misunderstood, this made me feel frustrated and angry.

My breakdown should not have led to such an extreme course of events, apparently there is a procedure which offers a lot more support than I experienced before the police were called. Had it happened midweek there would have been full support and care on offer from home. It's a shame it all happened on a Sunday! That said it happened and I am back to believing that everything happens for a reason, my reason was to share this nightmare by way of this book.

The panic and anxiety still pops in to say 'hello', even in my everyday life, I am hoping it will clear soon so I can feel my balance again and start to do more with my life. I'm back at yoga and back to my daily walking routines and magical baths.

It's been a cathartic process re-living what happened as I share the words here with you.

My next intention is to get this book out into the world. I have called the angels to support me.

I hope that by reading my story people will be able to have a deeper understanding of how it actually feels to go through something like this.

I hope that the system can change and maybe this book can be a catalyst to help move those much needed changes along as soon as possible.

We are living in a world which is evolving at super speed and we have to keep up with it.

It can be hard at times.

Hopefully this has helped you too.

Most who have been in my situation aren't able to speak up, they need support and don't always have it and that's really sad. Some even feel they have to take their own lives after experiencing the ordeal of the Mental Health System, something has to change!

Maybe things will get worse before they get better. I really hope not.

I would love for the whole system to be updated, I hope that by opening up myself and sharing my story it will help this process of much needed evolution.

It's time for us to join together and support each other. No more fighting what is, I've been there and done that over this last few months with all of the anguish and fighting in my mind. It doesn't help anyone in the long run, it creates dis....ease. It's time for positive change!

Let's be pro peace, pro love, pro support and most of all pro positive change!

WE CAN DO IT!

TOGETHER WE CAN CHANGE THE WORLD ONE STEP AT A TIME!

I ask a few things of you here today:

Next time you see a stranger on the street who looks fed up give them your best reassuring smile, you never know it might just change their day.

Next time you are going to online post some over hyped news about the awful stuff happening in the world think about who might see it and how it will affect them.

Next time you think you know what's going off in someone's head, take a step back and do your best to feel into what they are experiencing offering a helping hand wherever possible.

Focus on yourself as much as possible and say no when things feel too much, fill up your own cup first and foremost.

Always get plenty of sleep and rest when you feel tired rather than taking on more stuff in life.

Trust yourself more, listen to your inner guidance and wisdom.

Be conscious of what you are 'offloading' on others and don't drain people's energy, they may be running on empty.

Look after your loved ones like they are the most precious things in your life, because they are.

Look after yourself like you are the most precious thing in your life, because you are.

We all are!

Life is a precious gift and so are we.

All my love,

Liz

PS ~ Remember to love yourself no matter what! I'm doing my best to do that too!

Learn more about Liz here ~ www.liz-green.com